MONEY ON THE HOOF

by
Edith Wharton Taylor

Introduction
Ben K. Green

THE OLD ARMY PRESS

TIMES

SOME

1513 Welch
Fort Collins, Colorado 80521

Introduction
Ben K. Green

[over]

T. B. Saunders & Co.s' division of pens on the Ft. Worth Stockyards in 1931, operated by Tom B. Saunders III, second from right in group by booth. Other cattle buyers from left to right are: Jerry Ralls, Joe Garrett, Jim Stevenson, Saunders and Tom Hawkins. Courtesy, T. B. Saunders III

Introduction

MONEY ON THE HOOF — SOMETIMES has been well and interestingly written by Edith Wharton Taylor from extensive research of authentic sources. The author has portrayed the development of the livestock marketing industry in the North Central Texas area with special attention given to the developing of the Fort Worth Stock Yards and packing houses.

This research material has been brought alive by interviews with several of the surviving livestock operators who were there when the Fort Worth Stock Yards was in its infancy. Much of this material would never have been brought to light and put in print had it not been for the painstaking efforts of the author and those who contributed their knowledge and experiences.

Mrs. Taylor is an excellent historian who has given us a much needed book on the development of the marketing of livestock which has not been heretofore recorded and is a welcome addition to Texanna.

Ben K. Green
March, 1974

Contents

Years of Growth — From Trail to Rail

The first cattle in Texas were of Spanish origin. The Spaniards who moved into Texas brought their cattle and mustangs with them.[1] Cattle raising was important as a food source for early Texas settlers. Stephen Austin's group of colonizers developed herds which grew partly from stock that had gone wild. This was probably not the only source, however, as Austin's settlers had to kill wild horses to supply colonies on the Colorado and Brazos rivers with meat.[2] As settlers filtered in from the eastern and southern United States, they brought cattle of Scottish, English, and French origin with them.[3] The Governor of Texas made an addition to Stephen Austin's code of Civil and Criminal Regulations

Descendants of typical longhorn steers that were driven up the Texas Eastern [that intersected the Chisholm trail in Oklahoma] and Western trails to northern railheads. [The picture was made on the Saunders ranch of Parker Co. Texas in 1971.] Courtesy, T. B. Saunders III

when he insisted that these cattle carry a brand to indicate ownership. He required stock owners to register the chosen mark with the office of the alcalde.[4] Interbreeding of cattle took place, but the most abundant genes came from Mexican stock which gave the tough, touchy and productive Texas longhorn. its distinctive characteristics on (and off) the hoof.[5] The price of beef was good. Fat cattle sold for $18.00 a head in 1833, and the herds were on the increase. "Almonte in his report to the Mexican government said there were 25,000 head in the department of the Brazos and 50,000 in the department of Nacogdoches." Herds were growing in the Austin area too. Then along came the revolution; and the cattle herds, which so conveniently solved a problem of logistics for both armies, were considerably reduced. Besides eating the beef, General Filisola tried to drive cattle into Mexico ahead of his retreating army. Some of these longhorns got away or were never caught; and these cattle formed wild herds in the region between the Neuces and the Rio Grande.[6]

Texas is rich in streams and rivers which generally flow from the northwest to the southeast, since this is the way the state's three giant steps are tilted. The northwestern step or High Plain is separated from the Central Plains by outcroppings of the Cap Rock and the Upper Colo-

3

rado River. The southeastern step of the Coastal Plain is separated from the middle step by high rolling hills and mountains and the timber breaks along the rivers.[7] Anglo-American cattle ranching probably began on the edge of the coastal plain at Victoria; and cattle probably increased and spread out along the banks of rivers and streams which provided water, grass, shade trees, and brushy protection. They increased along the way to San Antonio and they moved on to the Edwards Plateau which borders the southern edge of the Central Plain. From there they went North and West.[8]

After the end of the War with Mexico, the longhorn herds began to multiply producing unbranded cattle which could be had by any claimer tough enough to take them. There was no money on the hoof then because there was no market. The California Gold Rush in 1849 appeared to be a solution to this problem. The first trail blazed from the cattle ranches of South Texas to the gold fields of California was headed by James Ellison.[9] For a few years, thousands of cattle were driven West through El Paso to California. Enough survived the hardships of terrain and Indian attacks to make the venture profitable.[10] Less dangerous but more wasteful was the practice of slaughtering cattle for their hides and tallow only. Boats carried these products from

4

plants on the coast to the eastern United States. This practice died out after the Civil War.[11] The cattle business was slowly spreading across Texas, and by the middle of the nineteenth century, Texans had established their domain as the great cattle state in the Union.[12] As the Indians were removed or migrated to other areas during the 1850's, cattle operations spread to East Texas which was at a time when another and more accessible market opened up in New Orleans. Not only was this market closer, but delivery was comparatively simple as the beeves were shipped by boat. The success of both the California and New Orleans markets were short-lived as the rigors of the trail West were too costly and the buyers in New Orleans began to quibble about the quality of Texas longhorn beef. Texans began to check the distance North to the Union Pacific railroad and to consider other markets for their cattle.

While the Forty-niners streamed West to get rich in the California gold fields, Camp Worth struggled into existence on the banks of the Trinity River. Although the little community was an army outpost, Camp Worth never actually functioned as a Fort. Mrs. Arnold, wife of the post commander, was the first woman to come to the fort. Capt. Edward S. Terrell was the first settler, and he came to trade with the Indians. Only a

5

handful of settlers remained on September 17, 1853 when the army left, but from the beginning the citizens of this abandoned post on the Trinity were ambitious and public spirited. Eighteen fifty-six was a big year for the community. That was the year when Fort Worth stole Birdville's booze and bought itself the county seat for Tarrant in the ballot box.[14] This same year, the stagecoach linked Fort Worth's 200 inhabitants with the outside world.[15] The Fort Worth Whig Chief, the city's first newspaper was established, and it may have begun publication in time to announce the birth of the city's first boy, Howard W. Peak.[16] It was about this time that cattlemen in the southern part of Texas began looking North for a market to sell their beef on the hoof, and the citizens of Fort Worth began looking for ways to attract more people and more money. Included in the group with spirit and vision were James H. Ellis, G. P. Farmer, E. M. Daggett, C. M. Peak, John Peter Smith, and B. B. Paddock. The county government enticed more people to settle in Fort Worth, and most of them apparently rallied to the support of the city promoters and their enterprises.[17] E. M. Daggett bought the cavalry stable and converted it into a hotel in 1853.[18] During the next seven years, other businesses also struggled into existence in this frontier town. Then the Civil War erupted and interrupted the plans of Texas cattlemen

Old settlers and the dates they came to Fort Worth. Top row, left to right: Howard W. Peak, 1856; Capt. J. C. Terrell, 1857; Dan Parker, 1858. Bottom row, left to right: Capt. Sam Woody, 1850; Capt. Ed Terrell, 1843; Richard King, 1854. Courtesy, Fort Worth Public Library

Land Agency. House lots and farms for sale and rent. Courtesy, Fort Worth Public Library

and Fort Worth promoters. From 1861-1865, there was almost no cattle trading in Texas; and with a decline in population, due to the war, the only stores that were still in business by 1866 were those that could furnish supplies for cattlemen and trail drivers.[19]

In 1866, the first of the great trail herds began to move up from South Texas. Many of the cattle moved through Fort Worth on their way to a railhead in Kansas. The prices Texas cattle brought in the East barely paid shipping expenses from Kansas, but the following year showed a slowly improving market.[20] In the post-Civil War cattle business, a man had to be tough enough to survive the financial gamble as well as the rigors of the trail.[21]

> *Right after the war cattle was all they had, and no market or no railroads for them. These old Boys drove 'em north till they found markets and buyers, and it was through their efforts that the whole Northwest was stocked with cattle. The only revenue that come into this whole country for years was just what was brought back by these old "Waddies."*[22]

Texans quickly turned cash receipts, from the meat-hungry North and East, into staples and equipment for their ranches.[23] As prices improved, more cattle moved across Texas blazing new trails as drovers went in search of other markets. Between 1866 and 1870, 250,000 cattle trailed North.[24] Fort Worth's first native born male says that "the Chisholm Trail proper started near San Angelo, crossed the Pews River at 'Horse Head Crossing', and branched, one prong going to New Mexico, the other through the Indian Territory, now Oklahoma."[25] But W. Saunders, who was President of the Old Trail Drivers' Association insisted that the famous Chisholm route never entered Texas.

The Chisholm Trail was marked from Abilene, Kansas to Red River station and no further. It was started by Hoe McCoy, building of the stock-yards at Abilene and McCoy hired Chisholm to lay out the route. The trail was marked by furrows plowed with ox-team, across the plains and trees blazed through the timber.

At times so many herds would be on the trail they would spread out on either side and some herds went all the way to Abilene without being actually on the trail except occasionally.

There were hundreds of cattle trails in Texas, but all running north led into either the eastern or western cattle trail and the eastern trail led to Red River station where the Chisholm trail began.[26]

Mr. Saunders suggests that the reason so many old trail drivers and others insisted that the Chisholm Trail was a Texas route was because it connected with a Texas trail of which there were four main ones: the Eastern trail, two Western trails, and the Goodnight-Loving trail. Ten million cattle and 1,000,000 horses traveled over these four cattle trails between 1866 and 1895 for an amount totaling $250,000,000. There were many other trails in Texas besides those four and they led to sixteen other states — as far West as California and as far North as North Dakota. "All cattle trails leading from the Kansas markets to the northwestern range were called, The Texas Cattle Trails."[27] The drives over these trails were often referred to as steer drives because this class was the most numerous and most popular. Bulls were disruptive to herds and poor to eat unless processed by a packer. Cows, unless barren, often had a calf to nurse which meant they were slow on the trail; and they needed more and better grass than steers to hold their own weight. Steers could travel faster than cows; and if grass was good and plentiful, they could even gain

10

weight on the trail during this period of drives to northern markets.[28]

Fort Worth was the last town of any size in the vicinity of the eastern trail which sometimes passed along side of and sometimes went right through this village of the 1870's.[29] Blessed with plenty of good grass and fine water, it became a natural stopping place during the drive North.[30] Trail-weary cowboys could buy supplies and relax and forget the heat, dust and sweat of the trail, the monotony of driving from dawn until dusk and the loneliness of night herding. New businesses sprang up in Fort Worth to cater to the needs and whims of cowboys. Saloons and gambling halls opened and the number of hotels increased to quarter cattle buyers who now maintained offices in Fort Worth in order to meet the trail drovers and purchase their cattle as they came through town. A few citizens were apparently shocked by the wide-open reputation that this particular queen of the prairies was gaining; but most town supporters seemed to believe that any business which profited Fort Worth was good business.[31] During 1870, cattle prices were good, and 300,000 head were driven to Kansas. That year the railroads cut shipping prices in an effort to ruin each other which increased the profits of cattle dealers.[32] Tales of a prosperous drive reached home by late autumn, and the next

11

View of the Public Square. Fort Worth, Texas. ca. 1877. Courtesy, Fort Worth Public Library

"During Paddock's Time" "Mulkey Boys" Courtesy, Fort Worth Public Library

spring 600,000 head of Texas cattle hit the trails as drovers urged them towards Kansas.[33] Buyers there were not as eager to purchase beef as in 1870, however, because they had already purchased corn-fed beef from the Middle West States. Farm cattle fared better than the Texas longhorn when in competition for buyers. Beeves which were not bought were left to winter in Kansas on already close-cropped ranges. The winter was severe and thousands of cattle died. As a result, in 1872, the number of Texas cattle involved in a drive dropped back to the 1870 figure of 300,000 head.[34]

Eighteen seventy-three was another significant year in the history of Fort Worth and the development of the cattle market. The town grew from about 500 people in the fall of 1872 to 3 or 4,000 people during 1873.[35] Since the 1850's, city promoters had been trying to attract the railroads.[36] By 1873, the Texas and Pacific had completed that part of the track which ran sixty miles from Shreveport to Longview; and the railroad construction company had graded another two hundred miles — putting them to within twenty-four miles of Fort Worth.[37] The editor of the *Democrat* published a map on the front page of his paper depicting Fort Worth as the future railroad center of Texas.[38] The approach of the Texas and Pacific railroad attracted many settlers who wanted to cash in on the growth and development of the marketing of livestock in the town.[39] Another railroad company began construction of the Trans-Continental line which was to run from Sherman to Fort Worth, and cattle dealers hoped that a railroad would get to town in time for the summer cattle trade.[40] B. B. Paddock encouraged Texas families to quit following their herds over Texas cattle trails, and settle down to a life of farming and cattle ranching.[41] He urged railroad construction companies to hurry and bring their roads to Fort Worth, a town of excellent location, beautiful climate and fertile soil.[42] The Texas legislature considered granting a new railroad charter to a line to be called the Fort Worth Waco Southwestern.[43] Northern cattle buyers set up operations at Fort Worth as the city seemed to be attracting the railroads which could convert it to a shipping center for cattle from all over the state.[44] "Hell's Half-Acre" grew with the rest of the town. Gamblers conducted their business openly, and thugs and robbers contributed to the rough reputation that the town was continuing to gain.[45] Conscious of growth and in a spirit of reform, Fort Worth decided to clean up the town a little and organize for a lot more business. The citizens wrote the first charter, and the 13th Texas Legislature approved it. As of March 1, 1873, Fort Worth was incorporated. On April 3, Dr. W. P. Burts was elected the first mayor.[46] But the railroad did not get to Fort Worth that year, so 400,000 Texas cattle trailed to the railheads in Kansas.[47] Then on September first, almost twenty years after the army had left Fort Worth, dreary news of the failure of Jay Cooke and Company in Philadelphia reached Fort Worth. Cattle buyers were apathetic. The beef market slumped. Fort Worth dwindled to less than one thousand people. As people left the dying town construction stopped, businesses closed, and commerce halted. Only those who had no choice stayed to try and survive on the business brought by the cattle drive in the spring of 1874. And only those with strength and imagination stayed to try and make Fort Worth grow into a meat shipping and packing center. For awhile there was no development.[48] "The grass literally grew in the streets;"[49] and hogs were free to root there and to wallow in the mud when the rains came.[50] The price for cattle stayed around two dollars per hundred weight through 1875. Low prices brought Texas cattlemen to the realization that they needed to improve their breed.[51] Texas longhorns had gained a reputation for being the original bearers of the fever tick which caused splenetic fever in cattle and was often fatal to all breeds.[52] Northern buyers began to discriminate against Texas cattle for this reason. Also, the long horns on Texas cattle limited the number of stock that could be loaded into a

16

cattle car making it costly to ship this breed on the hoof.[53]

During this highly speculative period in which discrimination against ticky cattle was based upon an intuitive hunch rather than scientific investigation, Mr. Glidden came up with perhaps the best possible way to stop the spread of Texas fever, and make it profitable for ranchers to import registered stock to upgrade their herds. But there is no indication that he had this goal in mind when he opened his factory in De-Kalb, Illinois. There were several inventors of barbed wire that applied for patents at approximately the same time as Mr. Glidden.[54] The idea spread quickly as inventors demonstrated the effectiveness of their particular design.[55] Glidden's original idea, however, resulted in the production of the best, most practical and most popular type of barbed wire. After receiving his patent, Glidden contacted John W. "Bet-A-Million" Gates who got barbed wire sales rolling in Texas. At first store keepers were reluctant to handle the strange new wire, and cattle owners who were not yet land owners were against erecting fences.[56] However, the year 1875 marked a decline in cattle trail driving and an increase in ranch land fencing.[57] "Barbed wire ended the open range and revolutionized the cattle business."[58] It was the beginning of the end for the Texas Longhorn.

17

Gradually, the miles of track shortened the distance between Fort Worth and a rail head. The trail became less important to all save those who resented the freight charges and weight losses on cattle shipped by rail.[59] Those citizens who had been working to make Fort Worth a terminus for one of the railroads being built westward since 1858, and who saw their dreams submerged in the chaos of the Civil War and the financial panic of 1873, now worked with renewed enthusiasm.[60] The Texas and Pacific Railroad had until July, 1874 to complete construction of the track to Fort Worth. The Texas Legislature granted a time extension in May, 1873.[61] By December of that year, the line had been completed only to Texarkana, and once again the construction company asked the Texas Legislature for a time extension.[62] The citizens of Fort Worth were somewhat divided in their support of the work on the Texas and Pacific Line by 1874, when the T&P submitted yet another time extension request. One group in the city was unalterably opposed to granting any concession to the construction company of the Texas and Pacific. Another and less dynamic group was in favor of granting any time extension that the company demanded rather than risk incurring their animosity. The largest group in the city held firmly to a sensible middle course of granting time extensions in exchange for investment protection and assurances

18

that the line would soon be completed.[65] But more delays during 1874 and the beginning of 1875 encouraged Fort Worth's men and women to take more positive action. They undertook the extension of the T&P by investing their money, labor, material and supplies in the completion of the line to Fort Worth. They organized the Tarrant County Construction Company which began work by the fall of 1875.[64] As Riche Brothers and Tierney struggled to complete the T&P before "the adjournment of the first legislature held under the new state constitution" of 1875, some visionaries began to consider the impact train transportation would have upon the marketing of cattle in Fort Worth. B. B. Paddock extolled the advantages a beef packing business could expect to find in Fort Worth such as excellent water and plenty of herding grounds. In an editorial in *The Democrat,* he urged the businessmen of Fort Worth to get busy and secure at least one meat packing firm. He suggested that with the arrival of the Texas and Pacific and other major railroad lines, that Fort Worth was especially well situated in the heart of good ranch land to serve as a meat processing center for the entire southwest.[65] During 1875, *The Democrat* adopted the policy of publishing a weekly list of herds that passed through Fort Worth during the cattle drive season. Information included the names of cattle owners, the size of the herds and the type of cat-

19

tle. Fort Worth continued to outfit trail drovers as it worked to bring the railroads to the city. When the Texas Legislature convened in January of 1876, the T&P once again asked for a time extension. But the Legislature was determined that the T&P must have the line completed to Fort Worth prior to adjournment or lose a land grant of 16 sections per mile voted the T&P by the 1872 Legislature. By July the Senate was pressing for adjournment, but the House blocked the adjournment resolution. Tarrant County's representative, Nicholas Henry Darnell kept the Legislature in session for a critical 15 days by voting against adjournment. With the arrival of the first train on July 19, 1876, the rail replaced the trail in importance in the development of the cattle market in Fort Worth.[66] During the 80's, Fort Worth became an important railroad center, and by the end of that decade the city was served by eleven trunk lines. The three railroads radiating from Fort Worth which proved most important to the development of the country were the Texas and Pacific, the Fort Worth and Denver City, and the Fort Worth and Rio Grande. These three lines opened up country which was excellently suited for the development of cattle ranches through fencing. The Fort Worth and Denver City line connected the gulf with Colorado and the northwest on March 14, 1888. This railroad had a favorable effect on the cattle industry in

Locomotive #20 of the Texas & Pacific Railway, the first locomotive to pull a train into Fort Worth in 1876. From an original drawing by Mr. Ronnie Rasor, retired draftsman of the Texas & Pacific Railway. Courtesy, Texas & Pacific Railway Co.

the Panhandle and cattlemen found it a cheap and easy way to send their stock to market.[67] But the Texas and Pacific carried the first train load of cattle from Fort Worth; and E. M. Bud Daggett, future senior member of Daggett-Keen Commission Company was on hand in the fall of 1876 to help load out the shipment from the Texas and Pacific yards.[68] Train transportation ushered in a new phase in the marketing of livestock in Texas, but there were still some nagging problems connected with the cattle business. Although the long horns of Texas cattle limited by perhaps five head the maximum number that could be shipped in a car, this was not serious.[69] And although the prices didn't necessarily suit all cattlemen, many apparently favored the rail over the trail. More serious was the problem of the Texas Fever Tick which caused northern buyers to discriminate against Texas cattle. The invention of the refrigerator car in 1868, "made it possible to establish packing houses at railroad points near cattle producing centers and transport meat in refrigerator cars to the big consuming centers."[70] All of these reasons combined to encourage cattlemen to view with favor the establishment of a meat processing plant, and Fort Worth was ideally situated for this purpose.

About the time that Fort Worth was being abandoned by the Army, Bradford Grimes was

22

experimenting with a meat packing operation on Trespalacios Creek in South Texas. The warm weather and the lack of refrigeration precluded a successful operation. Apparently the stench soon grew so severe that the pioneer packer was forced to quit.[71] Twenty-two years later on April 25, 1875, *The Democrat* predicted that Fort Worth would become a large producer of refrigerated meats for export.

A man named Richardson first went to Dallas for the purpose of establishing a meat packing plant in that city. Dallas was not interested, but the editor of the Fort Worth Democrat *got wind of the proposal and hastened to Dallas to meet Mr. Richardson. He offered Richardson six acres of his choice, which was all the land that the man wanted, to establish a meat packing plant in Fort Worth. Mr. Richardson made his selection. Fortunately the land belonged to John Peter Smith and it was only necessary to tell Smith what was in the wind and the deed was forthcoming. He erected a small packing plant on the land now occupied by the Brewley Flouring Mills. As Richardson only essayed to kill and refrigerate hogs, and as there were very few hogs in Texas, the plant was short lived. He soon sold it and went out near Cisco and put in a plant to make plaster from gypsum.*

Shortly after this a man by the name of Higgs came to the city and in a few days secured capital to erect a refrigerating plant in the southeast part of the city. He killed a cargo of cattle and sent them to St. Louis, but that proved like sending coals to Newcastle, and his venture was doomed to failure. He sold his plant to Mr. Issac Dahlman of the firm of Dahlman Bros., the first clothing merchants in the city. He killed cattle and sent them to Liverpool by way of Galveston, but they were so long on the way that they did not arrive in good condition. This ended the third attempt, but did not dismay the people of Fort Worth. They believed that this was to become a packing house center, and in 1890 thirty men got together and agreed to put in $1,000 each and purchase some lands and put up more money, share and share alike, as it was needed. Mr. H. C. Holloway was selected to manage the affairs of the company, and he bought lands where the present plants are situated and proceeded to build fences and lots and later on a small packing house. It had a capacity of 250 cattle and 1,000 hogs per day. About this time John R. Hoxie

24

came to Fort Worth from Chicago, and as it was thought he knew all about the industry he was induced to put in more money, buy more land and increase the capacity of the yards.

He too made a failure, and the plant after a precarious existence was sold to Messrs. Simpson and Niles of Boston, neither of whom were practical packers. Mr. Niles was a business man, and under his management, with the assistance of Mr. Harvey A. Judd, still a citizen of Fort Worth, the plant earned money. The owners recognized the fact that the plant did not meet the requirements of the times, and with the assistance of some of the public spirited people of the city they enlisted the interests of Armour & Co. and Swift & Co. and secured the establishment of these concerns. Most of the thirty men who put the first money into the plant surrendered their holdings to make the deal go through.

The corner stones of the buildings were laid on the 13th of March, 1902, in the presence of a large concourse of the citizens of the city. Just a year thereafter the first cattle were slaughtered. The packing plants, stock yards, horse and mule barns, hog and sheep *pen cover (ed) an area of about 100 acres.* [72]

By the 1900's, Texas cattle had been upgraded through fencing off land for the purpose of developing cattle ranches; and an experimental tick control program was inplemented to stop the spread of Texas Tick Fever. Fort Worth had been successful in her bid to attract the major railroad lines to this city in the heart of the cattle ranch country; and Fort Worth also attracted major packers — Armour and Swift. These factors assured the success of Fort Worth as a center for the marketing of livestock.

Main Street from 7th, Fort Worth. Dec. 11th, 1896. Courtesy, Fort Worth Public Library

Trader's National Bank, Fort Worth, Texas. [Feb. 18, 1886] Courtesy, Fort Worth Public Library

[1]C. L. Douglas, *Cattle Kings of Texas* (Fort Worth: Branch-Smith, Inc., 1939), pp. 3-7.

[2]*The Fort Worth Press* - 1936. "Texas Centennial Scrap Book Edition," p. 2, (available in East Texas State University Library).

[3]Douglas, *Cattle Kings of Texas,* pp. 4-5.

[4]"Texas Centennial Scrap Book Edition," p. 2.

[5]Douglas, *Cattle Kings of Texas,* p. 5.

[6]"Texas Centennial Scrap Book Edition," p. 2.

[7]*Texas In 3-D,* 1st Edition, 1969, Kistler Graphics Inc., Denver, Colorado.

[8]Stanley Walker, *Texas* (New York: The Viking Press, 1961), pp. 81-82.

[9]Douglas, *Cattle Kings of Texas,* pp. 5-6.

[10]B. B. Paddock, *Fort Worth and the Texas Northwest* (4 vols.; Chicago: The Lewis Publishing Company, 1922), II, p. 526.

[11]"Farm and Ranch," Fort Worth's First 100 Years, p. 2. *Fort Worth Star-Telegram,* October 30, 1949.

[12]Paddock, *Texas and the Texas Northwest,* II, p. 526.

[13]Douglas, *Cattle Kings of Texas,* p. 7.

[14]"Texas Centennial Scrap Book Edition," [n.p.].

[15]Robert Harris Talber, *Cowtown-Metropolis* (Fort Worth: Texas Christian University, 1956), pp. 1-2.

[16]Howard W. Peak, *The Story of Old Fort Worth.* [n.p.; n.pub., n.d.] Available in the archives of the Fort Worth Public Library.

[17]Buckley B. Paddock, *Early Days in Fort Worth, Much of Which I Saw and Part of Which I Was.* [n.p., n.pub., n.d.] Available in the archives of the Fort Worth Public Library.

[18]"Texas Centennial Scrap Book Edition," [n.p.].

[19]Research Data Project (Available in the Fort Worth Public Library).

[20]Douglas, *Cattle Kings of Texas,* pp. 269-70.

[21]"Farm and Ranch," Fort Worth's First 100 Years, p. 2.

29

[22]Will Rogers, "Rogers Visits the Old Range," Copyright 1926 by McNaught Syndicate, Inc.

[23]Paddock, *The Democrat,* April 25, 1875, p. 3.

[24]"Farm and Ranch," Fort Worth's First 100 Years, p. 2.

[25]Peak, *The Story of Old Fort Worth.*

[26]Resolution passed at the Old Trail Drivers' Association meeting in San Antonio, 1931 or 1932.

[27]Geo. W. Saunders, from text of article prepared by the President, Old Trail Drivers' Assoc. Courtesy of his grand nephew, Tom Saunders.

[28]Ben K. Green, *Wild Cow Trails* (New York: Alfred A. Knopf, 1969), pp. 157-159.

[29]During October, 1971, Mr. Bryan Perkins of Barbers Book Store in Fort Worth related that a committee to consider the placement of a Texas Historical Marker at the site of the cattle crossing on the Trinity River ran into trouble when three cities were proposed, and arguments in support of the three claims were equally convincing. Finally, one site was selected to be marked; however, supporters for all three proposals may have been correct. Cattle that did not follow a trail exactly probably did not cross a river in just the same place every year.

[30]"Farm and Ranch," Fort Worth's First 100 years, p. 16.

[31]Paddock, *Early Days in Fort Worth,* p. 31.

[32]Paddock, *Fort Worth and the Texas Northwest,* II, p. 530.

[33]"Farm and Ranch," Fort Worth's First 100 Years, p. 2.

[34]Paddock, *Fort Worth and the Texas Northwest,* II p. 530.

[35]Paddock, *Early Days in Fort Worth,* p. 6.

[36]"Historical," Fort Worth's First 100 Years, p. 21.

[37]*The Democrat,* February 8, 1873, p. 3.

[38]Paddock, *Fort Worth and the Texas Northwest,* II, p. 514.

30

[39]"Transportation Section," Fort Worth's First 100 Years, p. 2.

[40]*The Democrat,* February 8, 1873, p. 3.

[41]*The Democrat,* January 25, 1873, p. 2.

[42]*The Democrat,* April 26, 1873, p. 4.

[43]*The Democrat,* March 1, 1873, p. 2.

[44]"Farm and Ranch," Fort Worth's First 100 Years, p. 16.

[45]Oliver Knight, *Fort Worth — Outpost on the Trinity* (Norman: University of Oklahoma Press, 1953), p. 87.

[46]"Historical," Fort Worth's First 100 Years, p. 21.

[47]Paddock, *Fort Worth and the Texas Northwest,* II, p. 530.

[48]Paddock, *Early Days in Fort Worth,* p. 6.

[49]*Ibid.,* p. 7.

[50]Knight, *Fort Worth — Outpost on the Trinity,* p. 116.

[51]Paddock, *Fort Worth and the Texas Northwest,* II, p. 533.

[52]"Tick Fever Studies Were a Boon to Mankind," *The Cattleman,* Vol. XVI, No. 10, March, 1930, p. 29.

[53]Talbert, *Cowtown — Metropolis,* p. 34.

[54]"Farm and Ranch," Fort Worth's First 100 Years, p. 16.

[55]"Transportation," Fort Worth's First 100 Years, p. 2.

[56]Henry D. and Frances T. McCallum, *The Wire That Fenced The West* (Norman: University of Oklahoma Press, 1965), p. 190.

[57]"Farm and Ranch," Fort Worth's First 100 Years, p. 16.

[58]Erwin E. Smith, *Life on the Texas Range,* Text by J. Evertts Haley (Austin: University of Texas Press, 1952), p. 69.

[59]McCallum, *The Wire that Fenced The West,* p. 191.

[60]Peak, *The Story of Old Forth Worth.*

[61]*The Democrat,* May 10, 1873, p. 3.

31

[62]*The Democrat,* December 14, 1873, p. 2.

[63]*The Democrat,* March 14, 1874, p. 1.

[64]"Transportation," Fort Worth's First 100 Years, p. 2.

[65]*The Democrat,* April 25, 1875, p. 3.

[66]"Transportation," Fort Worth's First 100 Years, p. 2.

[67]Paddock, *Fort Worth and the Texas Northwest,* II, p. 507-511. For a complete list of railroads centered at Fort Worth see page 516.

[68]Paddock, *Fort Worth and the Texas Northwest,* IV, p. 713.

[69]Dr. Ben K. Green. Interview at the Fort Worth Livestock Exchange, Fort Worth, Texas, October, 1971.

[70]"Farm and Ranch," Fort Worth's First 100 Years, p. 16.

[71]Douglas, *Cattle Kings of Texas,* p. 29.

[72]Paddock, *Fort Worth and the Texas Northwest,* II, p. 657-659. This account of the early trials and failures in attempting to make Fort Worth a meat packing center has apparently been paraphrased by writers interested in the succession of meat processing and packing facilities at Fort Worth from Richardson to Armour and Swift. As this material is central to the thesis, the author believes it will be helpful at this time to return to the apparent original source of so many authors.

Ticky Cattle, Texas Fever and Toppling Prices

Texas fever was a problem for Texas cattlemen until late in the 1930's.[1] Ticks spread the disease known as Texas or splenetic fever among cattle reducing the value of cattle and making it hard for Texas cattlemen to compete successfully for good prices at commercial stock yards.[2]

Texas fever was not peculiar to Texas. It existed on the continents of Africa, Asia, Australia and South America as splenetic fever. It was probably introduced to the continent of North American along with a shipload of cattle from Spain. Dr. Mease recognized the existence of the disease as early as November 3, 1814. In a lecture before the Philadelphia Society for Promoting Agriculture, he remarked that cattle had carried the disease from a county in South Carolina to a county in Pennsylvania. Virginia legislators also recognized the existence of this disease in 1814. During that year, the state of Virginia passed a law refusing to allow cattle from certain sections of South Carolina to pass through Virginia because they feared that ticky cattle were a threat to their livestock.[3] This reaction was based upon a suspicion of the tick as the cause of the fever, rather than upon scientific investigation of the tick and its relation to splenetic fever.[4]

During the 1860's, Texas fever spread to Illinois, Kentucky, and Mississippi. In some areas it reached epidemic proportions.[5] Serious study into the case of the disease was unproductive until well after the Civil War period. In the autumn of 1879, Dr. D. E. Salmon began a study of Texas fever. He became connected with the U.S. Department of Agriculture that same year, and by 1884 he had achieved the position of Chief of U.S. Bureau of Animal Industry. He suspected the tick, but he found no support for this suggestion from Professor Gamgee of England or J. R. Dodge, the statistician of the Department of Agriculture. These men were doing research on Texas fever; but it was not until the late 1880's that scientists proved that the tick was responsible for causing splenetic fever.[6]

34

Texas received further help in its fight against Texas fever when in 1888, Dr. Mark Francis became professor of Veterinary Science and chief veterinarian of the Texas Agricultural Experimental Station. Dr. Francis studied the tick and its relation to Texas fever, and he devoted much of his life to looking for a way to get rid of both.[7]

Texas cattle owners needed to get rid of the fever spreading tick so that they could reduce death losses in their herds and concentrate upon upgrading their cattle. Experimental fever tick eradication work and the use of fences on the range encouraged cattle owners to go to the effort and expenses of improving their herds. Tick eradication reduced losses very slowly before the turn of the century. With the discovery of barbed wire, fencing became practical on the open range, and tick infested cattle could not penetrate tick free herds that were kept enclosed by a fence.[8] The Lassator family was one of the first to import registered cattle into Texas. This family selected Short Horn Durhams from England and they landed them at Galveston, but Texans also favored Herefords and Red Poles. Such early efforts as this were experimental and did little to improve the quality of range stock.[9] After 1885, Texas embarked on a general program to improve the quality of Texas cattle by importing

35

registered bulls from England, Scotland and the Eastern United States.[10]

The study of Texas fever and its cause resulted in the creation of federal and state agencies and many laws designed to regulate the livestock industry.[11] In May, 1884, the 48th Congress approved an act to establish the Bureau of Animal Industry. The law sought to control the spread of contagious diseases among domestic animals by preventing the exporting and importing of diseased animals at both state and national levels.[12] During this same year, states neighboring Texas enacted legislation which protected themselves from tick infestation by discriminating against Texas stock. This made it difficult for cattlemen south of the Red River to sell their cattle outside of Texas.[13] The Quarantine Act of Kansas in 1884, for instance, prohibited Texas cattle from entering that state except during the period from December the first to March the first.[14] The stiffening of a Colorado law in 1885 further restricted the movement of Texas cattle.[15]

In 1893, lawmakers established The Texas Live Stock Sanitary Commission to provide effective control at the state level against the spreading of infectious and contagious diseases.[16] During this same year, the Federal Government established a national quarantine line which dis-

36

criminated against Texas (and southern) cattle. Texas fever ranked second among animal diseases in its virulence and diffusion for over half of a century, and an organized fight to halt the spread of this disease began at the great quarantine line.[17] The establishment of a Texas quarantine line in 1894 marks the beginning of the experimental period in tick eradication which lasted until 1906.[18] "This line started on the Oklahoma border between Collingsworth and Childress Counties and extended in a general southwesterly direction." The Federal Bureau of Animal Industry cooperated with the Texas Live Stock Sanitary Commission in a county by county inspection to discover which counties were infested with the fever carrying tick.[19] The federal government insisted that cattle being driven or shipped out of Texas in a northerly direction across the national quarantine line be dipped at least twice under government supervision in a tick-killing solution, or travel in marked cattle cars to indicate their ticky condition so that they would be dipped when unloaded at their destination. Even clean cattle which came from ticky areas had to be dipped.[20]

As northern buyers became more discriminating in their cattle purchases, Texas cattlemen began to consider the advantages of processing Texas beef prior to shipment out of the state.[21] Fort Worth became the meat packing center of the Southwest when, in 1902, Swift and Armour located plants adjacent to the Fort Worth Stock Yards.[22] Those ranchers with clean cattle ranging in a quarantined area now had an outlet with the establishment of a central market in Texas. The arrangement was also good for the packing houses as meat from south of the quarantine line which passed federal government inspection was cheaper by virtue of point of origin, and Swift and Armour took advantage of the difference in price.[23] Cattlemen from ticky areas had a reliable market at Fort Worth after 1902; and the public was protected from bad meat by law even before Swift and Armour set up meat processing plants in Fort Worth. On August 30, 1890, Congress provided for the inspection of meats requiring that they be stamped or marked in some way so as to identify a product as fit for import and export.[24] The Texas fever tick lived on cattle. It did not live on horses or other domestic animals. Federal government inspectors checked cattle which were not slaughtered unless free of Texas fever (and all other diseases.)[25]

Between 1894 and 1906, the Bureau of Animal Industry in cooperation with the Texas Live Stock Sanitary Commission devised two methods for ridding cattle ranges of ticks. One method was to vacate a range for a certain period.[26] Cattlemen objected to the expenses involved for it meant that no revenue could be earned from the vacated land. Another method was to dip cattle at regular intervals in a solution of arsenic. This treatment was experimental in that the contents of the solution and the percentage of ingredients was not definitely established at this time. [27]

Between 1906 and 1919, tick eradication work was voted upon by each infested county in Texas, [28] but there was no state or federal law forcing counties to comply with an eradication program during this period. Consequently, "In 1906, one-fourth of the total area under quarantine in the United States for tick infection was in Texas." Within the state of Texas, 73% of the total area was tick-infested. [29] The Texas Live Stock Sanitary Commission in cooperation with the Bureau of Animal Industry began tick eradication work in the infected counties of northwestern Texas. [30] While tick eradication work was being pushed on a county by county basis in Texas, research work was going on all over the South to discover the cheapest, safest, and most effective way of killing the fever tick. By 1910, work was becoming more systematized as Dr. Mark Francis, former dean of the School of Veterinary Medicine at Texas A&M, improved a dip which would kill the fever tick while doing minimum damage to cattle. [31] By 1912, dipping solutions and procedures were standardized in most Texas counties.[32] In northern and northwestern counties, where the tick population was scattered and the effort and money required to eliminate this parasite was not too great, counties usually voted to establish a tick kill program. In southern and southeastern counties, where the tick population soared in brushy and wooded areas, the effort and money required to eliminate this parasite was very great. Counties in this area were understandably slow to adopt a tick eradication program.[33] By 1914, the Chief Inspector of the Texas Live Stock Sanitary Commission could announce that 6,500 square miles of quarantined land had been released, and the Texas quarantine line had been adjusted accordingly.[34] The Chief Inspector of the Texas Live Stock Sanitary Commission in 1914, Mr. Wallace, recommended that all tick infested cattle be dipped at least twice a year even though an owner might not be planning to move his herd across the quarantine line. From observation and experience, he recommended using an arsenic solution which he insisted was both safe and effective.[35] George L. Abbot, a distributor for livestock medications, carried the Chief Inspector's claims further. In an advertisement for Cooper's Tixol Cattle Dip, he claimed that Tixol was "beneficial to Hair and Hide — Harmless to the Animals."[36] Cattle owners, however, were probably more interested in the claim

40

Gathering cattle to be dipped for fever ticks on Texas ranch. Courtesy, T. B. Saunders III

of a Mr. Blair in Tulsa than the claim of George L. Abbot. William Blair of Tulsa, Oklahoma asked for permission to present a claim against the federal government in 1915 because a Federal Government Inspector forced him to dip two thousand of his cattle, which were ready to be shipped to market. Apparently, the Federal Inspector could not find any evidence of ticks, and the cattle were going to market where they would be inspected prior to being slaughtered. After the dipping, many cattle showed evidence of being severly burned and a large number died. Mr. Blair sent a sample of the dipping solution to an analyst. He found that it contained two and a half times the required amount of arsenic. Mr. Blair's case became a test case "to test the liability of the government in this work as the damage and loss to Mr. Blair of Osage County was due to the careless mistake of the Inspector employed by the Federal Government." Naturally Mr. Blair wanted compensation and cattle owners followed the case with interest.[37]

By 1915, the Chief Inspector of the Texas Live Stock Sanitary Commission was urging all cattle owners to dip their cattle regularly throughout the year so that the work of tick eradication could be completed within a one year period. He offered to supply stockmen with bulletins which described how to construct a dipping vat, install a dripping pen, and how to get the best use out of both. He also presented an impressive set of figures to encourage cattlemen to join in the tick eradication program.[38] The editor of *The Cattleman,* A. C. Williams, joined the Chief Inspector, W. A. Wallace, with his own brand of encouragement when he asked his readers to "consider the tick and its high cost of living."[39] Dr. E. M. Nighbert of the Cattle Raisers Association of Texas had already appealed to the business sense in cattlemen in urging them to cooperate with a federal government sponsored program to control and eradicate ticks.[40] Dr. Nighbert compared the cost of treatment with the price of unquarantined beef in the market. He showed that the cost of lumber, hardware, iron work and concrete needed to build a chute, vat and dripping pen was cheap as compared to the cattle prices cattlemen from quarantined areas were forced to accept at a market.[41]

Not satisfied that dipping was the entire solution to the tick problem in Texas, Dr. Mark Francis continued to study the problem and experiment with other methods of tick eradication. Not all that he tried were successful. At some point during his research, Dr. Francis hit upon the idea of electrocuting ticks. He tied a steer securely, and then he wired him in such a way that an electrical current could pass through the brute in sufficient quantity to kill its ticks. When Dr. Francis turned on the current, the poor brute apparently went into convulsions. The ticks appeared unharmed by the experiment, but the steer dropped dead.[42]

Work to eradicate the tick by dipping went along satisfactorily as stock owners became more aware that tick-free cattle brought better prices. Transportation companies, bankers, commercial clubs, business men, cattle owners and state and federal authorities in the southern part of the state cooperated in a concerted effort to reduce the quarantine area of Texas by two-thirds in one year.[43] Swift and Armour bought beef from all areas of Texas. The packers at the Fort Worth Stock Yards purchased 267,439 cattle and 94,421 calves during the fiscal year ending June 30, 1915.[44] The Fort Worth Stock Yard Company advertised the advantages of shipping to a Texas market in the slogan, "A Shorter Haul - A Smaller Shrink - A Lower Freight - And Many Buyers."[45] During this same year, the Texas Panhandle, which had traditionally been a large scale producer of feeder cattle that were shipped to other states for finishing, shifted emphasis to raising feeder calves and finishing them themselves.[46] Breeders discovered that by feeding their cattle and finishing their improved stock themselves their improved cattle gained better in their

44

own feed lots and brought higher prices at market.[47] Dr. Francis made it profitable for breeders to import pure bred bulls to improve the quality of their herds when he developed a subcutaneous injection which produced immunity in cattle to fever tick infection. By early 1916, he had inoculated 396 head of high bred cattle which were valued at $100,000; and only one cow died as a result of the treatment.[48]

In 1916, the Texas Live Stock Sanitary Commission recommended dipping cattle every eighteen to twenty days beginning in the spring as early as possible after the tick dormant season ended and certainly no later than July first.[49] The United States Department of Agriculture issued new regulations that same year. As of July first, only the tick infested cattle intended for immediate slaughter could be shipped to interstate markets. Cattle not intended for slaughter had to be accompanied by a certificate of Federal inspection classifying them as tick free; or the cattle had to be dipped even though they were designated for shipment to states within the national quarantine area. The reason for this change in regulations was to keep ticks from reinfecting areas where eradication work was being carried on, or where it had been successfully completed but not finally inspected to remove it from the quarantine area.[50]

45

During the period from 1917 to 1919, tick eradication work received the greatest support from the southern part of Texas. The cattlemen from this area supported the Texas Live Stock Sanitary Commission and the Cattle Raisers Association of Texas in their effort to obstruct the passage of two bills in the Texas Legislature. The Sciter Floyd Bill in the Senate, and the Barnes Bertram Bill in the House sought to weaken the Texas tick eradication law of 1916. The East and North Texas cattlemen generally supported these bills as they feared a government tick control program.[51] They were an independent breed of men who did not want the government in their business. The 35th Texas Legislature gave the South Texas cattlemen a tick law with teeth in 1919 when they enacted the Zone Law. The Zone Law made dipping compulsory in every ticky county. These legislators divided the infested areas of Texas into three zones and assigned each zone a date upon which to begin compulsory dipping. The Northern Zone was to begin dipping that year. The Middle and Southern Zones were scheduled to begin dipping in 1920 and 1922 respectively.[52]

The North and East Texas cattlemen resisted compulsory dipping. Although cattle owners now knew that a certain kind of tick spread Texas fever, they professed a lack of confidence in the research that proved this fact and that established arsenic dip as a means of eradicating the tick. In actuality, these independent men who had never been forced by law to comply with a livestock regulation resented being forced to dip their cattle. They also resented the expense, and they dreaded rounding up their herds every three weeks. They understood the nature of a cow brute, and they knew that once a beast had been forced into a dipping vat and had felt its tender skin burn, that it would take a crew of men on horses to get the whole herd into a tank a second time.

Herd drivers drove the cattle to the vat where one man was stationed with a long pole. The chute at the entrance to the vat was wide enough to hold one animal at a time. The man with the pole had to prod the first into the vat. After he got the line of cattle moving, his job was to poke the head of each critter under the dipping solution. The animal was then permitted to exit the vat by a ramp. The other cattle generally entered the dip as long as they could see a beast exiting on the other side of the vat. The ramp out of the vat led to a cement bottomed dripping pen which was built on a slope so that the dip could drip off of the cattle and run back into the vat. The tick inspector's job was to test the percentage of ingredients in the dip and to see that the crew performed their duties properly. He did not have to test the dip if a veterinarian was present to do this. Tick inspectors issued certificates to cattle owners for shipping purposes or as part of the routine inspection at stock yards.

The entire dipping process was physically hard on cattle and caused them to shrink, which was another reason why stockmen opposed this treatment. Cattle owners faced a serious problem in the late fall after frost, for then the grass was no longer very nutritious, and it was extremely difficult for cattle to regain lost weight. In the spring, cattle were weak after having endured a rugged winter, and the weakest and oldest cattle would often die in the earliest dippings. Stock owners revolted periodically by filling vats, constructed by the County Commissioners Court, with barbed wire and broken glass and by dynamiting the dipping facilities; but despite these attacks, the dipping program continued.[53]

In July, 1920, the Chief of the Bureau of Animal Industry and the Chairman of the Live Stock Sanitary Commission combined their offices at Fort Worth. They did this in order to promote cooperation between the state and federal authorities in tick eradication.[54] Neighboring states put additional pressure upon Texas to get rid of fever ticks. The legislation which they

48

enacted may have furthered this cooperative effort as the market for tick infested cattle became more restricted. On June 11, 1921, the Maryland State Board of Agriculture barred the importation of cattle originating from any federal quarantine area because of Texas fever. North Carolina and the District of Columbia also put shippers on notice that they would no longer receive cattle from tick infested areas.[55] Oklahoma was next to enact an anti-tick cattle law. The legislators declared that after January 1, 1922, ticky cattle would not be allowed to pass through the State of Oklahoma without a dipping certificate which showed that livestock had been dipped ten days prior to shipment under the supervision of a federal or state inspector.[56] Louisiana and Arkansas followed Oklahoma in restricting the importation of ticky cattle into their respective states. The Arkansas law stated that, "the shipment of cattle from tick infested territory of Texas (or any other state) into or through Arkansas for any purpose, is prohibited until such cattle have been entirely cleaned of ticks and certified to by a recognized inspector of the Bureau of Animal Industry."[57] In 1922, Texas legislators stipulated that all cattle had to be certified tick free or would not be moved from quarantined areas.[58] There was a good reason for this new law. Since the inauguration of the Zone Law, it had become the custom to release quite a large area from quaran-

49

tine in Texas every fall. The released area, however, soon became reinfected because of the movements of ticky cattle from a quarantined area into a cleaned area.[59]

The fight against the fever tick was a long one in Texas, and it wasn't until the Texas legislature passed the Zone Law in 1919 that real progress was made in all of the state. This progress meant better prices at stock yards from fatter cattle. "In March, 1916, yearling steers weighed from 1,000 pounds to 1,250 pounds in Fort Worth, and in March, 1922, the same age steers weighed from 1,400 pounds to 1,650 pounds."[60] *The Cattleman,* always a supporter of tick eradication work, urged its readers still south of the quarantine line to get busy and clean up their area so that they too could improve the grade of their cattle and ship feeders to the Corn Belt. As the number of ticky cattle declined, the dairy cattle increased and by 1923 this latter group largely supplied packers with the cheaper grade of meat.[61] Also by 1923, only one-third of the total area of Texas was still under federal quarantine.[62] The compulsory tick eradication program saved the cattle industry in Texas.

[1]Dutch Voelkel. He spent his life in the livestock industry on the Fort Worth Livestock Exchange. Interview at the office of the *Livestock Reporter,* Fort Worth, Texas, June 24, 1971.

[2]Ted Gouldy, Editor of the *Livestock Reporter.* Interview at his office, Fort Worth, Texas, June 24, 1971.

[3]"Tick Fever Studies Were a Boon to Mankind," *The Cattleman,* Volume XVI, No. 10, March 1930, p. 29.

[4]B. B. Paddock, *Fort Worth and the Text Northwest* (4 vols.; Chicago: The Lewis Publishing Company, 1922), II, p. 528.

[5]Edward Everett Dale, *The Range Cattle Industry* (Norman, Oklahoma: University of Oklahoma Press, 1930), pp. 54-55.

[6]"Texas fever has the distinction of being the first disease caused by a microorganism proved to attack its victim exclusively through the agency of an intermediate host or carrier of its causitive germ or microparasite, and the Bureau of Animal Industry has the distinction of being the first institution to discover that a disease can be transmitted in this manner." This quotation is taken from "Tick Studies Were a Boon to Mankind," *The Cattleman,* p. 29. For a more complete discussion of the life and work of Daniel Elmer Salmon see *Who's Who In America* 1899-1900, p. 627.

[7]"Dr. Mark Francis," *The Cattleman,* Volume XXV, No. 4, September, 1938, p. 13. (For a more complete discussion of the work of Dr. Francis see *Who's Who in America.*)

[8]Paddock, *Fort Worth and the Texas Northwest,* II, pp. 536-538.

[9]Dr. Ben K. Green. Interview at the Fort Worth Livestock Exchange, Fort Worth, Texas, October, 1971.

[10]Paddock, *Fort Worth and the Texas Northwest,* II, p. 538.

[11]"Texas Campaign," *The Cattleman,* Volume IX, No. 1, June, 1922, p. 31.

[12]Public Law No. 41. Gilman G. Udell, Superintendent, Document Room, House of Representatives. U.S. Government Printing Office, Washington, D.C., 1971.

[13]Paddock, *Fort Worth and the Texas Northwest,* II, p. 528.

[14]Dale, *The Range Cattle Industry,* p. 69. Mr. Dale inaccurately states that the cause of Texas fever was unknown but that it was carried by Texas cattle, yet the period he gives above represents the dormant season of the tick. ˙

[15]*Ibid.,* p. 106.

[16]Dayton Moses, Jr., "Tick Eradication in Texas," *The Cattleman,* Volume VII, No. 10, March, 1921, p. 223. (Dayton Moses, Jr. was the chief clerk of the Live Stock Sanitary Commission of Texas.)

[17]Dr. E. M. Nighbert, "The Importance of Tick Eradication," *The Cattleman,* Volume I, No. 5, October, 1914, pp. 3-4.

[18]"Texas Campaign," *The Cattleman,* p. 31.

[19]Moses, "Tick Eradication in Texas," *The Cattleman,* p. 223.

[20]Dr. Ben K. Green. Interview at the Fort Worth Livestock Exchange, Fort Worth, Texas, October, 1971.

[21]Robert Harris Talbert, *Cowtown-Metropolis* (Fort Worth: Texas Christian University, 1956), p. 34.

[22]*Register,* Fort Worth, Texas. October 8, 1901, p. 11.

[23]Dutch Voelkel. Interview at the office of the *Livestock Reporter,* Fort Worth, Texas, June 24, 1971.

[24]Public Act. No. 247. Laws Relating to Agriculture. U.S. Government Printing Office, Washington, D.C., 1971.

[25]Bob Bramlett. Interview at the Fort Worth Livestock Exchange, Fort Worth, Texas, October, 1971. He has sold more sheep for the producer on consignment than any other man in the world.

[26]*The Weekly Citizen,* Fort Worth, Texas. May 18, 1906, p. 5.

[27]Tom Saunders. Interview at the Fort Worth Livestock

52

Exchange, Fort Worth, Texas, October, 1971. Tom Saunders III is the only son of the late Tom Saunders II who had the first brokerage firm on the Fort Worth Livestock Exchange. He has spent his entire life on the Fort Worth Stockyards.

[28]Moses, "Tick Eradication in Texas," *The Cattleman,* p. 223.

[29]J. E. Boog-Scott, "Fever Tick Eradication in Texas," *The Cattleman,* Volume X, No. 3, August, 1923, p. 41. (Mr. Boog)Scott was Chairman of the Live Stock Sanitary Commission at this time.)

[30]Dayton Moses, Jr., "Texas Begins Last Fever Tick Drive," *The Cattleman,* Volume VIII, No. 9, February, 1922, p. 15.

[31]*Fort Worth Livestock Reporter,* Fort Worth, Texas, December 16, 1910, p. 3.

[32]William Sim, "Tick Eradication at Texas A and M," *The Cattleman,* Volume IX, No. 8, January, 1923. (Mr. Sim was a Beef Cattle Herdsman at the Animal Husbandry Department of Texas A&M.)

[33]Ted Gouldy. Interview at the Fort Worth Livestock Exchange, Fort Worth, Texas, October, 1971.

[34]W. A. Wallace, "How to Get Best Results and Avoid Loss," *The Cattleman,* Volume I, No. 2, July, 1914, p. 6.

[35]*Ibid.* Mr. Wallace recommended using either ten pounds of 99% pure arsenic trioxide to 500 gallons of water or five gallons of Trixol to 500 gallons of water.

[36]*The Cattleman,* Volume I, No. 5, October, 1914, p. 36. Cooper's Tixol Cattle Dip was recognized by the U.S. Bureau of Animal Industry and the Texas Live Stock Sanitary Commission as being safe and effective.

[37]"Will Make Claim Against Government for Damage to Cattle Dipped by Federal Inspector," *The Cattleman,* Volume XI, No. 7, December, 1915, p. 17. In *Texas v. United States,* The U.S. Supreme Court established a precedent for the introduction of evidence which affected the ruling in two cases which were somewhat similar to the one

above. (See U.S. Supreme Court Decisions, Lawyer ed., Appeal and Error, Vol. 41.) Also see *Thornton v. United States,* Civil Court of Appeals, Fla. which set the precedent for *Carter v. United States,* Civil Court of Appeals, Ga. In both cases the court ruled against the claimants who filed against Inspectors of the Bureau of Animal Industry and the Federal Government. The *Corpus Juris Secundum* states that "In the protection of interstate commerce in cattle, the federal government had power to require domestic cattle to be treated in an effort to eradicate Texas fever." Vol. 15, pp. 614-615. Even though all those litigants had legitimate claims, the court denied them in each case.

[38]W. A. Wallace, "Tick Eradication — How to Avoid Loss From Dipping," *The Cattleman,* Volume II, No. 2, July, 1915, p. 5. "The total area of Texas is 262,290 square miles. Of this area, 96,000 square miles are above, and 166,290 square miles are below the State and Federal quarantine line. Of the 96,000 square miles above the State and Federal quarantine line, 27,000 square miles have been cleared of tick infection and released from quarantine since tick eradication began in 1907."

[39]"Consider the Tick — May be Eradicated by Systematic Dipping," *The Cattleman,* Volume XI, No. 3, p. 16, August, 1915.

[40]Dr. E. M. Nighbert from an address to the 38th annual convention of Cattle Raisers Association of Texas in 1914 as printed in *The Cattleman,* Volume I, No. 5, October, 1914, p. 3.

[41]"A Plan for a Dipping Vat," *The Cattleman,* Volume XI, No. 1, June, 1915, p. 17. This article is typical of several in *The Cattleman* during this period. It is more specific in giving specifications for building a vat and dripping pen than Dr. E. M. Nighbert, "The Importance of Tick Eradication," *The Cattleman,* p. 4.

[42]Dr. Ben K. Green. Interview at the Fort Worth Livestock Exchange, Fort Worth, Texas, October, 1971.

[43]"Work of the Bureau of Animal Industry," *The Fort Worth Daily Live Stock Reporter*, Volume XIX, No. 210, Tuesday, December 28, 1915, p. 2.

[44]Livestock report of the Fort Worth Stockyards Company for 1915.

[45]*The Cattleman*, Volume XI, No. 1, June, 1915, p. 6.

[46]Feeders refers to calves that were shipped north to be finished. The Panhandle began to grow milo and maize to feed their cattle crop so that shipping out of state was no longer necessary.

[47]"Panhandle Ranchmen Now Profiting By New Methods," *The Fort Worth Daily Live Stock Reporter*, Volume XIX, No. 206, Tuesday, December 21, 1915, p. 1.

[48]"Many Cattle Vaccinated at A&M College," *The Cattleman*, Volume XI, No. 11, April, 1916, p. 55.

[49]Dutch Voelkel. Interview at the Fort Worth Livestock Exchange, Fort Worth, Texas, october, 1971.

[50]"New Registration on Ticky Cattle," *The Cattleman*, Volume III, No. 2, July, 1916, p. 39.

[51]"Texas Tick Eradication Law Amended," *The Cattleman*, Volume VII, No. 1, June, 1920, p. 39.

[52]"Summary of Tick Eradication in Texas in 1922," *The Cattleman*, Volume IX, No. 8, January, 1923, p. 32.

[53]Dr. Ben K. Green. Interview at the Fort Worthy Livestock Exchange, Fort Worth, Texas, October, 1971. As a boy at home before and during the First World War, Dr. Green rode after the family cattle every eighteen days when the compulsory dipping program first began in Hunt and Hopkins counties of East Texas. Later Dr. Green was deeply involved in the tick business as a cattle trader on the Fort Worth stock yards, as a rancher in the late 1920's, and as a tick inspector for the Texas Live Stock Sanitary Commission in the early 1930's.

[54]Moses, "Tick Eradication in Texas," *The Cattleman*, p. 223.

[55]"Ticky Cattle Banned from Maryland by Board Or-

der," *The Cattleman,* Volume VIII, No. 3, August, 1921, p. 10.

[56]"Oklahoma Puts Ban on Movement of Ticky Cattle," *The Cattleman,* Volume VIII, No. 4, September, 1921, p. 33.

[57]"Tick Infested Cattle Banned by Arkansas," *The Cattleman,* Volume VIII, No. 7, December, 1921, p. 3.

[58]Moses, "Texas Begins Last Fever Tick Drive," *The Cattleman,* p. 15.

[59]Boog-Scott, "Fever Tick Eradication in Texas in 1923," *The Cattleman,* p. 4.

[60]Sim, "Tick Eradication at Texas A and M," *The Cattleman,* p. 15.

[61]Boog-Scott, "Fever Tick Eradication in Texas in 1923," *The Cattleman,* p. 43.

[62]*Ibid.,* p. 41.

Stockmen — A Special Breed of Gamblers

Aristotle said, "who sees things grow from their origin will have the most advantageous view of them." The following men worked at the Fort Worth Livestock Exchange. Some of them came to the stockyards soon after Armour and Swift built their plants in 1902. As this is the first internal study of the marketing of livestock at Fort Worth, a brief biographical statement about the men "who saw things grow from their origin" is pertinent to this study.

Tom Saunders went to work in his father's office in 1923. He is the son of T. B. Saunders, II, who was the first cattle dealer on the Fort Worth market in 1902. From 1910-1920, T. B.

57

Newly completed Livestock Exchange Building and Stockyards in 1903. Courtesy, T. B. Saunders III

Livestock Exchange Building, about 1945. Courtesy, T. B. Saunders III

T. B. Saunders & Co. Livestock Dealers [reputed to be the largest cattle dealers in the U.S.A. from 1910 thru 1920] office in the Ft. Worth Livestock Exchange Building in 1912. T. B. Saunders II, seated at desk by Lee Lytton. Standing is Lee Russell and Earl Baldridge. Behind counter is Roy Vanham, bookkeeper. Courtesy, T. B. Saunders III

Saunders & Co. handled more cattle than anyone else as order buyers, shippers and traders, and was considered the largest dealer in the United States. Tom Saunders was born in 1906, and he was at the stockyards every day until 1923. He closed the firm of T. B. Saunders & Co. in 1969. Vice-President and parade chairman of the Southwestern Livestock Exposition and Fat Stock Show, Tom Saunders, III has devoted much of his time and thought into preserving relics of old trail drivers, and memorabilia of cowboys and cattle, in a bunkhouse which he converted into a museum at his ranch southwest of Weatherford. His great uncle, George W. Saunders founded the commission company which bears his name. It is the oldest firm in Texas. George Saunders also organized and became president of the Trail Drivers Association of Texas.

Ted Gouldy moved with his family to Fort Worth in 1919, and started visiting the stock-yards when he was eight years old. He went to work for the *Fort Worth Star Telegram* as a live-stock reporter at the stockyards. He became edi-tor and publisher of the *Livestock Reporter* in 1933. It is the oldest and largest livestock publi-cation in the southwest. He has studied the buy-ing and selling of livestock during his entire adult life, and has spent eight years as organizer and manager of the Fort Worth Livestock Market

Institute, Inc.

Bob Bramlett went to work for Daggett-Keen Commission Co. in 1920. he started work in the hog yards of the Fort Worth stockyards. Later he sold his first load of sheep in 1925. At this writing, he has sold more sheep on consignment for producers than any other man in the world.

Dutch Voelkel went to work for "Uncle Bud" Daggett on the first of January, 1914. He started work in the hog yards. During the twenties, he became one of Tom Saunder's biggest cattle buyers. He started out on the stockyards when, in his own words, "you could trust everybody, and their word was enough." "Now," he says, "you can't trust anybody." Having spent his life in the livestock business, he has witnessed a history of triumphs and disasters in the marketing of livestock.

Ben Green went to work at the Fort Worth stockyards when in his teens. His job was to use his keen eye for conformation and size of livestock, and sort and group cattle into lots that would be most acceptable to a potential customer. But his principle interest in the livestock industry has always been in horses and mules. Before he turned twenty, he was driving herds of horses and mules from West Texas to the Fort

61

Bob Bramlett, Sheep Salesman. Courtesy, Texas Hereford Association

Ted Gouldy, editor and publisher of the Fort Worth *Livestock Reporter* **since 1933.**

"The day that I was twenty-one years old, I shipped some fat steers to the Fort Worth market that brought $5.10 a pound and weighed 1,060 pounds. It was such a good price and such good weight that I decided to dress up and take in the town."

Ben K. Green

Worth horse and mule market. Later, as a young man, Ben Green bought horses and mules on order as well as for his own speculation. He shipped his stock by train-lots to most of the southern states where Texas horses and mules were in demand.

The Fort Worth Stockyards Company of Fort Worth, Texas was established in 1902.[1] The packing houses of Swift and Armour were located at the center of almost one hundred acres of stock pens. As the flow of livestock increased over the years, the stockyards and the packing facilities of Armour and Swift expanded.[2]

The horse and mule market showed marked growth, and soon after 1902 became the leading horse and mule market in the nation.[3] Prior to United States entry into World War I, Europe became an important customer at the Fort Worth horse and mule market. Warring nations required many of these animals. During an eight month period in 1914-1915, the *Fort Worth Record* estimated that Europe purchased about 45,000 horses and mules and paid about $150.00 for each animal.[4] From 1916-1925, Fort Worth was the largest horse and mule market in the world. One of the reasons was that it was the only market that could supply cavalry and artillery type horses and mules in large enough supply

64

The first Ft. Worth Livestock Exchange Building and Stockyards — also Hotel, 1891. Location was near Niles City, where Armour and Swift Packing plants were later built. Courtesy, T. B. Saunders III

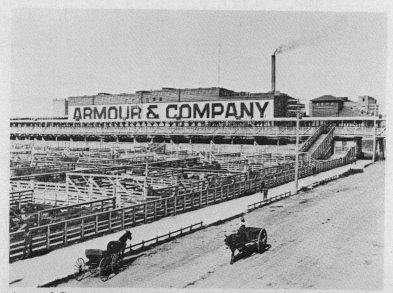

Armour & Co. packing plant at Ft. Worth, Texas, shortly after completion in 1903, showing parts of the overhead drive to plant and across Exchange Avenue to Swift Plant. Courtesy, T. B. Saunders III

for foreign countries as well as the United States. Another reason was that mules were cheaper to raise in the southwest because of an abundance of grazing land not found in the highly cultivated agricultural regions of the U.S. The light-boned breeds of horses comprised most of the horse population of the southwest, however, many breeders bred light brood-mares to draft stallions to produce what is known as a farm "chunk" which was also very useful as an artillery horse. Southern states were always customers of the Fort Worth mule market because their soils were light and their climate was hot during the growing season. Mules bred in the southwest withstood heat, insects and working conditions of the South better than the heavier type mules from Missouri and the mid-west. Another area of growth in the market was brought about by a demand for higher priced and finer mules to sell to tobacco and sugar cane growers in the South.[5]

The total horse and mule barns at Fort Worth had a capacity for approximately 4,000 head. The Stockyards part of the market had a capacity for 2,500 head of that total. The Burnett and Yount barns, the Ross barns and several commission firms comprised the horse and mule market at Fort Worth. The Burnett and Yount Barns were located several blocks north and west of the Livestock Exchange Building, and the Ross barns were situated across the street from the Spanish-styled structure. Sales were held on Mondays and Tuesdays of every week. They alternated between the two sale barns so that every week the location of the sale changed. Burnett and Yount quartered stock in frame barns that burned during a terrible fire in the late twenties which killed several hundred horses and mules. They rebuilt later. Ross Brothers kept stock in brick and cement structures which were part of the property owned by the Fort Worth Stockyards Company. Business was generally good between 1900-1935, but prices were highest during the depression and drought years of the thirties, and horses and mules continued to be bought and sold until the forties. The last government contracts were for mules for Italy and Guam during World War II. The crash in the horse and mule market came with recovery from the depression, for it was not until then that farmers could afford to replace workstock with tractors. Late in the forties, Fort Worth stopped having a horse and mule auction.[6]

Horses and mules were also important employees for the stockyards.

They were used to drive and pen cattle, horses and mules, and carry packer, stocker and feeder buyers and sellers each day through the thousands of animals being traded. These horses were also used in cutting and shaping up cattle for size, quality, sex and value. They were an indispensable part of the operation. [7]

The Fort Worth stockyard working horses soon gained an outstanding reputation as cutting horses. Men with the commission companies kept horses, ponies and mules in the yards at all times and they placed high value upon their individual mounts.[8] Commission men, packers, order buyers and stockyard employees usually rode horses,[9] but Dutch Voelkel rode a white mule which was born in 1940 and was given to him by a man in Oklahoma complete with Mexican saddle and blanket. The mule still lives on the Fort Worth stockyards, but he has now retired.[10]

The Fort Worth stockyards increased their hog business prior to and during World War I. Dutch Voelkel first worked in the hog yards when he started with Daggett-Keen Commission Co. In 1914, hogs were shipped in cattle cars. The floors of these cars were covered with mud. The hogs were loaded and shipped in such a fashion, that when they arrived at the Fort Worth stockyards no packer would bid on them until they were thoroughly hosed down. This was Dutch Voelkel's job, and he got ten dollars a week for it. He

68

spent four dollars on room and board which did not include a bath. This left him six dollars, some of which he spent at the barber shop where he could get a bath with a shave and haircut on Saturday night. Later sand was substituted for mud which eliminated a filthy situation.[11]

Six years later in 1920, Bob Bramlett went to work for Daggett-Keen Commission Co., and he also started in the hog yards. Between 1925-1930, Fort Worth was one of the best hog markets in the United States. It ran two or three dollars higher per hundred weight than Kansas City and Chicago, which was the big hog market. Western buyers passed up the heavier hogs of the other markets preferring the lighter finished hog at the Fort Worth market, which they could easily sell in California. This reason plus the fact that Texas did not produce enough hogs for local consumption and had to bring in hogs from Chicago and Kansas City, adding freight charges to the cost of the animal, kept the Fort Worth market consistently higher than the other hog markets in the United States. The fat on a hog was useless, except for lard, and the packers complained about the soft acorn-fed hogs until they developed a process for canning ham, which also eliminated the undesirability of the greenish cast of meat associated with peanut-fed hogs.[12]

By 1938, Swift and Armour could handle 9,400 hogs and refine 459,000 pounds of lard daily. Veal, lamb, mutton and beef did not require the extensive preparation and cutting that the hogs did. Hogs had to be scalded, divided into various cuts, chilled and then cured by sweet pickling, dry curing, or salting. The making of lard was another highly specialized process of refining, cooling, beating and canning. Packers knew that hogs had a higher percentage of usable material than beef or lamb, and that seventy percent of the animal could be eaten. Pepsin is an example of an important and edible by-product. This substance is found in the lining of the stomach of a pig, and is prescribed as an aid to digestion.[13]

Soon after 1930, the depression began to affect the price for hogs in all markets of the United States and even some in Europe. Washington instituted the "Government Hog-Kill, which went into effect at the Fort Worth market on August 28, 1934."[14] For five weeks, federally inspected packers purchased pigs from the commission firms at the Fort Worth Livestock Exchange with government money. Pigs which weighed less than 80 pounds were used for dehydrated animal products such as fertilizer, chicken feed and prepared hog feed. Hogs and sows which weighed over 80 pounds were turned into pork products, but

70

Group of buyers, yard boys, Commission Men and shippers in the Fort Worth Stockyards, posing on the back steps of the Fort Worth Livestock Exchange Building. Standing back row from left to right are: Dan Bellows, buyer for T. B. Saunders & Co., Ryan McMahan and Horace Wilson, Commission men. Rhome Shields, rancher from San Angelo, Texas and Bob Banner, hog and sheep salesman. 1915. Seated middle row, left to right: Max Bion, buyer for T. B. Saunders & Co., next unknown. Bottom row, Louis Kubitz, yard boy, Gainey Plaxio, T. B. Saunders & Co. buyer, unknown, and Bob Tadlock, dealer. Courtesy, T. B. Saunders III

An outlawed Texas Longhorn steer finally caught and shipped in to the Fort Worth Stockyards by George W. Saunders from his Medina ranch below San Antonio in 1904. Buyer for T. B. Saunders & Co. in background. Courtesy, T. B. Saunders III

these products were never put on the competitive retail market.[15] Hogs were never as important to the total livestock market at Fort Worth after this period. Those days in the twenties when thirty or forty cars of hogs would pour into the Fort Worth stockyards for days at a time were over.[16]

T. B. Saunders, II was the first order buyer on the Fort Worth stockyards in 1902. Most of his business was steer buying. During 1907-08 he bought large quantities of cattle that were shipped to Cuba. At this time, all cattle in the country were ticky, and the majority of the stockyards were tick yards. The native or clean part of the Fort Worth Stockyard was very small.[17] It was a little corner which had not been bricked, and which was separated from the selling side of the yard by a high board fence. The dipping vats were located here, and all cattle had to be dipped from one to three times depending upon the point of their origin and their condition when they arrived at the yards.[18] Dr. Victor A. Norgaard of the Bureau of Animal Industry, Washington, D.C. demonstrated the effectiveness of dipping cattle to kill splenetic fever-causing ticks on September 27, 1897 at the Fort Worth stockyards. Representatives of the Live Stock Sanitary Boards of Texas, Kansas, Illinois, Missouri, Nebraska, Oklahoma and Colorado witnessed the demonstration at Fort Worth. They were sufficiently impressed with the results to organize the Interstate Association of Live Stock Boards the next day. Cattlemen were also interested in the results because they knew that the price of Texas cattle would go up if they could successfully combat the tick.[19] After the packers established themselves at the stockyards, they took advantage of the difference in price between ticky and clean cattle. Sometimes the sellers paid a penalty as high as one-third of the regular market price on ticky cattle. At one time, cattle dropped to one penny per pound, which was the cheapest they ever were. Dutch Voelkel bought clean cattle at twenty-five cents a hundred which were from an infected area and had to be dipped. He penned them, gave them plenty of water, but he did not feed them. After a few days he sold them back for seventy-five cents a hundred. In this way, he capitalized upon the prejudice of buyers towards cattle from tick infested areas. A man by the name of Hicks found another way to take advantage of the tick situation. He owned a ranch north of Fort Worth where he could pasture herds of cattle for a price to drovers during the ten day period between the required dipping sessions at the Fort Worth Stockyards. If the ticks were all dead after the second treatment, the government inspector would permit the drovers to move their herds on to Oklahoma or some other state. During the 1920's, a lot of Texas still had

74

a tick problem, and the brushy east Texas area was not cleared up until the late 1930's, but they stopped dipping at the Fort Worth stockyards about 1930.[20] The drought and the depression of the thirties also accounted for very low cattle prices. Ben Green remembers when his cattle sold for as little as $2.00 a hundred weight, and Ted Gouldy remembers when a load of cattle that were sold on the yards brought only enough to pay for train freight, yardage fees and the commission. They did not bring enough, however, to pay for the hay they ate.[21]

There were several ways of moving stock to and from a terminal market. Use of the railroads was on the increase at Fort Worth after 1902. The charges for handling stock were low by present standards during the teens and twenties. The Livestock Exchange used to charge a handling fee by the car-load. During 1914-15 it was twelve dollars per rail car. Sometimes five or six shippers would take a railroad car together, and perhaps each shipper would load five or six cattle and then pro rate the freight charge. When the cattle arrived at the yard, they had to be sorted, weighed, penned and sold separately. The price for handling cattle shipped by rail rose to eighteen dollars per car later on.[22] Not all cattle arrived by rail. Until the thirties, cattlemen were still trailing their herds to the Fort Worth stock-

Texas and Pacific Union Station, 1902, on the occasion of a visit of West Texans to Fort Worth. Courtesy, Fort Worth Public Library

yards because it was sometimes cheaper and easier to drive stock than to put them on a railroad. For some ranchers, the distance to the railroad was as far or farther than the distance to the stockyards at Fort Worth.[23] The Fort Worth stockyards used to offer the services of a drover to cattle purchasers. If the distance was not great enough to necessitate shipment by rail, a cattle buyer could hire either one of two men named Sledge or Betts to drive cattle from the yards to the ranch. These two men were in competition with each other, which was to the advantage of the ranchers and cattlemen. One drover would always under-bid the other out of pure malice giving the cattle buyer an opportunity to move his purchased cattle at a good price.[24] T. B. Saunders, II invented another way to move cattle. During 1918, he grazed cows and calves on the west side of town in a pasture now called Ridglea Addition. He wanted to bring his cattle to market, but the town had grown considerably in the intervening years since he had first made Fort Worth his base of operations, and he was now confronted with the problem of how to get his stock to the stockyards. He had noticed flat-bed trucks, which were being used to haul furniture and later barrels of beer. He got a truck, ran a fence around the bed and loaded it with calves. Most of these were calves weighing less than 200 pounds and the ranch hands could load them by hand. The development of this method began a new era in the shipment of cattle for the plan was a success and soon caught on. A Fort Worth paper headlined the story the next day: "The Early Bird Gets The Worm." The account explained how cattle were shipped by "auto-truck," and that this was the first time that such a method was devised and used.[25]

The cattle market grew by volume of livestock handled, but with intermittent slumps in prices from 1910 through the dry depression years of the thirties.[26]

PACKERS' PURCHASE FOR FORTY YEARS

Years	Cattle	Calves	Hogs	Sheep
1902	4,776	11	55,183	357
1903	225,095	40,184	128,934	50,160
1904	289,964	85,237	267,870	46,052
1905	324,458	159,066	439,877	47,481
1906	342,804	225,854	512,616	67,042
1907	391,619	227,549	444,261	64,110
1908	453,869	191,165	652,259	69,237
1909	474,373	210,264	834,259	91,719
1910	435,435	204,353	505,321	92,768
1911	347,188	147,577	513,922	121,807
1912	356,990	179,399	339,307	188,281
1913	415,829	141,899	343,720	242,212
1914	481,483	139,484	460,862	295,689

1915	267,439	94,421	391,408	201,220
1916	312,102	152,539	860,050	189,343
1917	583,443	407,880	796,680	143,810
1918	529,375	431,663	568,223	130,677
1919	409,989	318,713	463,641	163,925
1920	308,043	251,532	322,194	206,447
1921	217,515	294,703	250,688	167,360
1922	242,604	290,518	372,466	67,095
1923	389,579	340,076	332,542	157,521
1924	479,563	421,233	314,281	180,499
1925	456,755	447,286	266,237	139,006
1926	401,292	284,320	175,318	237,878
1927	409,124	356,063	283,931	222,881
1928	374,278	340,171	387,051	207,323
1929	312,444	277,545	344,631	295,278
1930	272,206	220,478	244,393	228,211
1931	275,787	155,019	192,382	838,527
1932	216,667	112,519	235,744	909,512
1933	222,703	146,164	477,745	534,357
1934	245,008	182,579	380,609	292,151
1935	366,254	246,301	263,314	445,717
1936	332,062	201,334	308,611	423,782
1937	441,568	231,894	272,085	816,111
1938	316,563	159,489	191,298	865,954
1939	235,223	150,423	228,502	518,886
1940	220,651	135,986	313,647	700,978
1941	289,746	134,666	380,776	580,317

Total	13,680,366	8,786,555	15,116,838	11,241,681

About 1914, Joe McCarthy was steer buyer for Armour & Co., and Burt O'Connell was steer buyer for Swift. The steer buyer was the head cattle buyer over the cow and calf buyer.[27] During the period from 1910 to 1920, the Fort Worth Livestock Exchange handled approxmately 175,-000 cattle per year. Until the mid-twenties, these cattle tended to have more stretch to them than modern varieties, and the over-all quality was not nearly so good as more recently developed stock. Beef brought the highest price on record (excluding the market price of the seventies) early in the growth of the cattle market.[28] The first cattle to bring ten cents per pound were sold in 1916. These animals were ranged near the shipping points of Cresson and McFarland in Parker County, and were fed with cottonseed cake. After the United States entered World War I, the packers paid more for cake-fed cattle. Herbert Graves sold this type of stock to Wilson and Company, packers at Oklahoma City, for 12½ cents per pound.[29] The first yearlings to bring 10 cents per pound were sold at Fort Worth during 1919 or 1920.[30] After World War I, beef prices began to return to pre-war levels. In the process, prices fluctuated and were generally poor making it a stormy year for the meat producer. The packers did not buy up meat to protect the market as they had done in the past. During one good trading period in June, there was a shortage

80

of stock cars and the railroads were unable to meet the demands of ranchers bent on shipping cattle during a good selling period. Some stock went to market on the hoof, however, while many cattle did not make the trip at all, which must have been an advantage to those ranchers who did get their stock to Fort Worth.[31]

The 67th Congress approved the Packers and Stockyard Act of 1921, which was published by the U.S. Department of Agriculture, on August 15th. It went into effect at Fort Worth on January 18, 1922. It was enacted "to regulate interstate and foreign commerce in livestock." It provided rules for the care of livestock and their handling, feeding, watering and transport in the yards. It regulated the manner in which purchases were made. It outlined procedures for commission men, buyers, packers, and sellers. Among the specified services it discussed was that of weighing stock. This act described in detail the type of scales to be used, and it stressed the need for competent and honest employees to operate them.[32] "The most important facet of this new regulation, however, with regard to its effect on the Fort Worth Stockyards Company, was the mandatory divorce of packing companies from all financial interest in and/or control of the operations of stockyards and retail outlets."[33] Swift and Armour sold their interests in the Fort

Worth Stockyards Company and all other stockyards companies in order to comply with the law.[34]

The market fluctuated. Conditions ranged from moderate to turbulent. Operations were continual, however, for seven decades. The market began to build back to the pre-war high of 1917 in the early twenties. By the beginning of 1924, the *Fort Worth Livestock Reporter* could claim that packers were buying the greatest volume of cattle since 1918. During 1923, Swift and Armour bought 728,655 head of cattle and calves. Packer buying was up. So were packer complaints about the high cost of beef. Some people believed costs were high because the price schedule was unrealistic.[35] By 1925, packers were buying more calves than they had in 1917, and they were buying more cattle than they had since 1919.[36] Just before the depression hit the stockyards in 1929, Tom Saunders, II died. During the depression market conditions changed. Problems involving the marketing of livestock compounded when the drought of 1933-34 scorched Texas. Soaring temperatures caused stock prices to plummet. Grasslands dried up, and stock losses reached disturbing proportions. Many ranchers went bankrupt. Customers who used to buy 500 or 600 cattle at a time from T. B. Saunders & Co. could now buy only 50 or 60 head. In

1538 head bought by government during drouth of 1934 and assembled on Fort Worth Stockyards. Bought at prices ranging from $14.00 to $17.00 per head. Courtesy, T. B. Saunders III

order to survive this period of hardship, Tom Saunders, III decided in 1933 to start a clearing business. He began operations with Sam Graves, a man twenty years older than himself who was glad to take care of the office work. As Tom Saunders preferred to remain in the country this suited him very well. He selected ten men to go with him and buy cattle.[37] In this way he was able to keep up the volume of his trade in livestock.[38] The big runs in the cattle business occurred right after World War I and again in the thirties. During this period of bad times and low prices, more cattle came to the Fort Worth stockyards than at any other time in its history.[39] Daggett and Keen might have eight cattle cars on the yards at one time,[40] and there were days when there were as many as 15,000 cattle. The yards were full and trains had to wait to unload more cattle. The government acted under a drought emergency relief plan to buy up the stock that was pouring into the stockyards at Fort Worth.[41] The government and packing house purchases of meat caused livestock receipts to increase.[42] Rain relieved conditions on August 24, 1934.[43] The firm of T. B. Saunders & Co. cleared a lot of cattle between 1935 and 1948. In the early years of Tom Saunders' clearing business, his ten buyers might each purchase fifty head of cattle so that the firm would accumulate about five hundred cattle per day. By 1941, the firm had en-

Four year old cottonseed cake on grass fattened, steers driven from Lazy Open A ranch and penned by T. B. Saunders III owner and Olden Glenn, ranch foreman, in Parsons' switch railroad stockpens west of Fort Worth for shipment to Stockyards, during summer of 1930. Courtesy, T. B. Saunders III

larged and opened an office in Houston. T. B. Saunders & Co. cleared cattle for thirty-eight dealers on the Fort Worth stockyards and fifteen dealers at Houston. Now dealers for T. B. Saunders & Co. were buying two thousand to three thousand cattle per day. The firm made the most money in the clearing business during the depression years. Tom Saunders charged fifteen cents per head clearance while cattle sold for an average of twenty dollars each. He quit the business in 1969 when he was charging forty cents clearance and cattle were averaging one hundred and forty dollars per head. Interest charges in the thirties amounted to 3½% to 4%. Interest charges in 1969 had skyrocketed to 8½% or 9%.[44] It took seven or eight times as much money to handle cattle in 1940 as it did back in 1932 and 1933,[45] but business continued to be good and the firm of T. B. Saunders & Co. cleared over 300,000 cattle a year during the forties, nearly doubling the figure of the early twenties.[46] During a discussion of record high prices in the cattle market, Dutch Voelkel recalled that he creep-fed calves in 1950. They weighed a bit over 550 pounds and brought $35.60.[47] Tom Saunders remembered that steer yearlings reached an all-time high in 1952 for that decade. They weighed 700 pounds and brought $38.50. In 1971, they climbed higher weighing 400 pounds and bringing $41.50. During April, 1971 at the Abilene

86

market, steers weighing 296 pounds brought $56.65, and heifers weighing 287 pounds brought $47.00.[48] The only sure thing about the prices on the cattle market was that they fluctuated. They still do. To withstand the triumphs and disasters, a stockman had to be an innate gambler then and now.

The best sheep years were those from 1937-1947. Lamb sales peaked in 1943-1945. During those years, the Fort Worth stockyards sold over two million sheep. It was the largest sheep market in the United States. The biggest run that the yards ever had for one day was 59,000 sheep. Daily runs averaged 30,000 to 40,000 in the peak years. By 1946, the total sheep receipts may have dropped under two million, but it was still a good year.

Until the forties, stockmen sent sheep to the stockyards by rail. Shippers loaded sheep in double-decked cattle cars, and their competitiveness was so detrimental to the stock on board, their shipping business was eventually curtailed. A sheep rancher at Roswell, New Mexico, for example, might load his stock on the Santa Fe at Lovington. Rather than shorten the trip for the sheep by transferring them to another and more direct line while en route, the Santa Fe would keep them on their line for the entire journey although it might take a week to get to the Fort Worth stockyards. By the time the train finally arrived, many sheep would be crippled and some would be dead. It is for this reason that more sheep arrived by truck than by train during the forties.[49]

The government set a limit of how much the meat packers could pay for sheep, but they did not set a limit on the number of hours a buyer might work.[50] Bob Bramlett used to get home at 10:00 or 11:00 o'clock at night. After a shave and a bath, he lay down for a nap. By 2:00 a.m., there was a buyer from Armour, Swift or individual buyers on his front porch seeking the first chance to buy the sheep that Bob Bramlett had to sell for that day. Bill Johnson of American Meat Co. on the California coast was a regular customer. He shipped 2,500 old crop lambs weighing 80 to 110 pounds every morning. Bob Bramlett generally had 6,000 or 7,000 lambs to show Bill Johnson, who could pay $2.00 or $2.50 per hundred weight more for sheep than the packers could. The kind of sheep that the Fort Worth market generally dealt in were old ewes or fat lambs.[51] Delaine and Rambolet sheep used to be popular. The wool from this variety was good but very kinky. Bob Bramlett first promoted the Delaine spring lamb which he got from Fredricksburg and Kerrville, and which he sold for 6½

88

cents per pound. Gradually stockmen improved sheep by cross-breeding to the Rambolet and later the Suffolk.

The cheapest price that sheep ever brought was a penny a pound. Seventy pound ewes brought seventy cents, which did not cover freight or handling charges.[52] Sheep brought the highest prices after World War II. A herd averaging 95 pounds brought $32.50 per hundred weight. The type of sheep sold in the forties was not what is now selling in Fort Worth.[53] Top quality lambs today are cross-bred. These crosses produce a medium grade wool, and top quality lamb.[54]

"In 1900 the value of horses and mules in the United States totaled more than that of all the cattle, sheep, goats and hogs on the farms and ranches in the United States."[55] For this reason, it is not hard to understand why the Fort Worth horse and mule market, which showed early potential, grew to be the largest of its kind in the world, but perhaps the men in this market were the greatest gamblers among all dealers in stock, for although their market was situated in the heart of excellent grazing ranch land, they had no by-products to fall back on. Traders determined the value of their stock by its soundness, size and quality and what power it could furnish. The presence of packing houses effected their business little if at all. Dealers in hogs, sheep, and cattle bought and sold by the pound as well as by the head. These animals produced lard, wool and hides as well as meat. The horse and mule dealer dealt in the live animal only but each kind of market had its hay days at Fort Worth, and all of them eventually declined. The weak, who could not stand it when things got stormy, washed away with the ebb and flow of stock receipts. But the strong who stood hitched through the squalls and the blights of the most unpredictable of all types and kinds of markets added the "guts" which makes the glamour of cowboy trails live on to touch the memory of modern man.

[1]Taken from the 40th Annual Livestock Report of the Fort Worth Stockyards Company for 1941 with a summary for the years 1902-1941.

[2]By 1938, the Fort Worth stockyards had a capacity for 37,000 cattle and calves, 20,000 sheep, 20,000 hogs and 5,000 horses and mules. There were more pens, alleys and better facilities by 1938. From Fort Worth Chamber of Commerce.

[3]B. B. Paddock, *Fort Worth and the Texas Northwest* (4 vols.: Chicago: The Lewis Publishing Company, 1922), II, pp. 661-664.

[4]*Fort Worth Record,* July 29, 1915.

[5]Ben K. Green, *Horse Tradin'* (New York: Alfred A. Knopf, 1967), Preface.

[6]Ben K. Green. Interview at the Fort Worth Livestock Exchange, Fort Worth, Texas, October, 1971. (Horses were never included in any kind of government program.)

[7]Tom Saunders with Jane Pattie, "Equinine Employes," *The Cattleman,* Vol. LVI, No. 4, September, 1970, p. 53.

[8]Ben K. Green. Interview at the office of the *Livestock Reporter,* Fort Worth, Texas, June 24, 1971.

[9]*Ibid.*

[10]Dutch Voelkel. Interview at the office of the *Livestock Reporter,* Fort Worth, Texas, June 24, 1971.

[11]*Ibid.*

[12]Bob Bramlett and Ted Gouldy. Interview at the office of the *Livestock Reporter,* Fort Worth, Texas, June 24, 1971.

[13]Fort Worth Chamber of Commerce publication for 1938. Available in archives of library at ETSU. (Page 14 gives incorrect information in regards to the origin of Pepsin.)

[14]Milton C. Royles, "The Stockyards Story," (n.d., n.p., n.pub.). Available at the Fort Worth Chamber of Commerce. (It contains several inaccuracies and the reader should check the information included in this report care-

fully.)

[15]*Ibid.*, (n.p.).

[16]Bob Bramlett. Interview at the office of the *Livestock Reporter*, Fort Worth, Texas, June 24, 1971.

[17]Tom Saunders. Interview at the office of the *Livestock Reporter*, Fort Worth, Texas, June 24, 1971.

[18]Dutch Voelkel. Interview at the office of the *Livestock Reporter*, Fort Worth, Texas, June 24, 1971.

[19]"Farm and Ranch," Fort Worth's First 100 Years, p. 2.

[20]Dutch Voelkel. Interview at the office of the *Livestock Reporter*, Fort Worth, Texas, June 24, 1971.

[21]Ben K. Green and Ted Gouldy. Interview at the office of the *Livestock Reporter*, Fort Worth, Texas, June 24, 1971.

[22]There are a lot of additional charges in 1972. For example, it costs about $1.50 per head for selling, $1.50 per head for stockyard yardage, 8 cents per head for the meat board, and there is also a charge for brand inspection. The total cost for each animal now adds up to $4.50 or $5.00 per head for grown cattle and $3.00 per head for calves. For the services of the Fort Worth stockyards with reference to cattle, sheep, hogs, horses and mules refer to *The Livestock Hotel*, a publication of charm and interest put out by the Fort Worth Stockyards Company. The text is written by Ed C. Walsh and illustrated by N. M. Davidson during the period when A. G. Donovan was president, i.e. about 1941.

[23]Dutch Voelkel. Interview at the office of the *Livestock Reporter*, Fort Worth, Texas, June 24, 1971.

[24]Saunders and Pattie, "Equine Employes," *The Cattleman*, p. 63. These two drovers kept crews of riders to help with the movement of stock.

[25]Tom Saunders. Interview at the office of the *Livestock Reporter*, Fort Worth, Texas, June 24, 1971. Tom Saunders, II died in 1929. The flag on the stockyards was lowered to half mast. This was the first time that a man associ-

92

ated with the Livestock Exchange at Fort Worth was so honored.

[26]The above chart is reprinted from the Fort Worth Stock Yards Company 40th Annual Livestock Report for 1941. It includes a summary of the years 1902-1941.

[27]Dutch Voelkel. Interview at the office of the *Livestock Reporter,* Fort Worth, Texas, June 24, 1971.

[28]Tom Saunders. Interview at the office of the *Livestock Reporter,* Fort Worth, Texas, June 24, 1971.

[29]Dutch Voelkel. Interview at the office of the *Livestock Reporter,* Fort Worth, Texas, June 24, 1971.

[30]Tom Saunders. Interview at the office of the *Livestock Reporter,* Fort Worth, Texas, June 24, 1971.

[31]*Fort Worth Daily Live Stock Reporter,* Volume XXV, January 1, 1921, p. 1. (The name of this newspaper undergoes slight modification through the years, which accounts for the variation in the footnotes which cite this newspaper.

[32]Public Law No. 51. Gilman G. Udell, Superintendent, Document Room, House of Representatives. U.S. Government Printing Office, Washington, D.C., 1971.

[33]Royles, "The Stockyards Story."

[34]*Ibid.*

[35]*Fort Worth Daily Live Stock Reporter,* Volume XXVIII, Saturday, January 26, 1924, p. 1.

[36]See chart on p. 78 of this manuscript entitled "Packers' Purchases For Forty Years".

[37]Dutch Voelkel was one of Tom Saunders' cattle buyers.

[38]Tom Saunders. Interview at the office of the *Livestock Reporter,* Fort Worth, Texas, June 24, 1971.

[39]Ben K. Green. Interview at the office of the *Livestock Reporter,* Fort Worth, Texas, June 24, 1971.

[40]Bob Bramlett. Interview at the office of the *Livestock Reporter,* Fort Worth, Texas, June 24, 1971.

[41]Dutch Voelkel. Interview at the office of the *Livestock Reporter,* Fort Worth, Texas, June 24, 1971.

[42]Tom Saunders. Interview at the office of the *Livestock Reporter*, Fort Worth, Texas, June 24, 1971.

[43]*Fort Worth Democrat*, August 25, 1934, p. 1.

[44]Tom Saunders. Interview at the office of the *Livestock Reporter*, Fort Worth, Texas, June 24, 1971.

[45]Dutch Voelkel. Interview at the office of the *Livestock Reporter*, Fort Worth, Texas, June 24, 1971.

[46]Tom Saunders. Interview at the office of the *Livestock Reporter*, Fort Worth, Texas, June 24, 1971.

[47]Dutch Voelkel. Interview at the office of the *Livestock Reporter*, Fort Worth, Texas, June 24, 1971.

[48]In other words, the average price at that market and at that time was $169.00 per head.

[49]Bob Bramlett. Interview at the office of the *Livestock Reporter*, Fort Worth, Texas, June 24, 1971.

[50]Ben K. Green. Interview at the office of the *Livestock Reporter*, Fort Worth, Texas, June 24, 1971.

[51]This is a slaughter class of sheep.

[52]When so informed, one shipper explained that he had no more money, but that he would be glad to send more sheep.

[53]Bob Bramlett. Interview at the office of the *Livestock Reporter*, Fort Worth, Texas, June 24, 1971.

[54]Ben K. Green. Interview at the office of the *Livestock Reporter*, Fort Worth, Texas, June 24, 1971.

[55]Green, *Horse Tradin'*, Preface.

The Central Market — Its Strengths and its Weaknesses

During the embryonic phase of the meat packing industry, slaughter houses operated independently from packers. These were generally small, rural, unsanitary and wasteful operations. The farmer-slaughterer usually worked on the banks of a stream in a corner of his farm. He kept hogs penned beneath the floor of his slaughter house to eat up what was not of commercial value. Other wastes were disposed of in the stream. The packer packed beef or pork with salt in barrels and cured bacon and hams in his smoke house. The packer operated in cold weather only until mechanical refrigeration was invented. This method of operation was as old as the nation, and it was not until such men as Swift and Armour became interested in the process that a central livestock market began to form and grow.[1]

P. D. Armour and John Plankinton formed a partnership to establish a market for livestock in Milwaukee. Their operation included stock-yards, a slaughtering area and meat packing facilities. Business was good so Armour and Plankinton built plants at Kansas City and Chicago, and on December 25, 1865, The Union Stock Yards of Chicago were opened for business. By 1875, Armour was ready to make Chicago his permanent base of operations, but his partner Plankinton wished to remain in Milwaukee, so the partnership was dissolved. There were seven or eight stockyards scattered around Chiago before Armour arrived, and he consolidated the slaughtering and meat packing business, but he continued to use the same methods which had been employed before the American Revolution.[2]

During 1875 Gustavus Swift arrived in Chicago to set up a livestock purchasing business, buying western steers to ship to the eastern market. Apparently that part of the Chicago River which served Armour's slaughter and packing houses, and which was aptly called Bubbly Creek, served to jog Swift into finding a more efficient, sanitary and practical way of shipping his beef to the East. The operations of slaughtering and packing meat were combined by Armour. With the arrival of Swift and the invention of refrigeration, the operation grew to industrial size when packers updated procedures. The term, no longer descriptive of the method employed, remained and this new industry was designated the meat packing industry.[3] The big packers developed markets at Kansas City, Omaha, St. Louis, St. Joseph, Sioux City and St. Paul to handle the flow of stock from west to east and to bring in more cash receipts for their companies.[4]

In 1890, about thirty citizens of Fort Worth subscribed $10,000 each to found the Union Stockyards Co. of Fort Worth. L. V. Niles, a businessman from Sommerville, Massachusetts, became the manager. When the citizens realized they needed a big packer to establish a plant in order to add profits to their plans, they agreed to surrender their holdings in the company in order to attract Armour, who was interested in the Fort Worth venture. Swift got wind of the deal and he also became interested. Niles got together with both packers, and in 1902 Swift and Armour built packing plants at the end of Exchange Avenue.[5] To honor vision, genius and success, the area which included stockyards and packing plants was christened Niles City. It was incorporated so as to remain free of Fort Worth jurisdiction, and by 1911 became the richest per capita community in the United States. Fort Worth finally annexed Niles City after a lengthy court battle in 1922.[6]

After the Packers and Stockyard Act of 1921 forced a divorce between packers and the Union Stockyards Company, ". . . a corporation formed in Chicago initiated public ownership of the yards, removing ownership from Fort Worth. Later more stock was accumulated by Union Stockyards Co. and the Fort Worth Stock Yards became in 1944 a division of United Stockyards, now owned by Canal-Randolph Corp., with headquarters in New York."[7]

During the Second World War, the U.S. government bought practically all the meat that the big packers produced. Concurrent with this change in the market, the big packers closed their branch plants around the country. The consumer in a small or medium-sized town had no place to get meat, as the big packers could not supply him. This created an opening for small, independently owned packing plants to establish themselves. They grew bigger and more efficient and eventually got government inspection and grading of their products. In this way, a trend towards decentralization of the marketing of livestock and the meat packing industry was re-born.

98

Livestock auction barns began to appear all over Texas. For a long time, the auction people and the terminal market people disagreed as to whether to ignore. or join the trend.[8] Charges of malpractice gave the auction people a propaganda weapon. A few commision firms engaged in both order-buying and selling, using a customer as a customer by selling to one customer while buying from another customer at the same time.[9] The Packers and Stockyards Act of 1921 which was supposed to have regulated that sort of malpractice was not entirely successful.

The auction supporters maintained that they operated a strong competitive market. They argued that transportation costs were moderate, that the buyer or seller could expect assistance at an auction through close personal contact with the market men, that it was easier for a farmer to buy livestock locally than on a terminal market, and that auction barns were closer to shippers' homes.[10] This last argument was perhaps the best because a farmer could take his calves to an auction to run through the ring in a matter of hours. If the calves did not bring the price the seller wanted he could take them home and the cows would probably take them back having never missed them. If a seller had to go to Fort Worth from a distance he would have a long haul or freight expense. He would also have yardage and other fees deducted from the sale, weight loss and time loss if he accompanied his stock. After a day or two at the yards, the cows would probably not take back the farmers' calves forcing the stockmen to accept the price bid on his stock.[11]

The terminal market people maintained that they had greater buying power. They argued that they were a more competitive market than an auction market, that they provided facilities to feed, rest and handle large numbers of stock, that they maintained fulltime state and federal employees to regulate the sale of stock, that they could offer dipping, vaccination, and similar services, that they maintained hourly contact with other large livestock markets, and that their volume of business made them a price basing point for a large area.[12] One of the most important advantages of the central terminal market was its power to bargain with the government in Washington.[13] A case in point centered upon the grading of Texas lambs. Texas stockmen generally produced old crop Rambolet lambs.[14] The government inspectors decided to grade these lambs as mutton. Ignoring the guidelines for distinguishing lamb from mutton they graded only on the look of the meat.[15] One inspector explained the new guideline by saying that it was like looking at a pretty girl. If he liked what he saw he

100

graded it lamb, and if he did not like the looks of the meat he graded it mutton. Texas lamb producers became indignant over this issue as the difference in price between lamb and mutton was considerable. Ted Gouldy published the story in the *Daily Livestock Reporter* under the banner line, "A Lamb Has To Be Like a Pretty Girl." That got results. Lyndon Johnson, who was then majority leader of the Senate and controlled the purse strings of the Department of Agriculture, came to the rescue. Soon after publication of the story, the government graders returned to the proper guidelines for grading lamb.[16]

Although by the end of World War II decentralization of the marketing of livestock had become a trend, and stock sales and meat packing were localized, the United Stockyards Corporation chose to ignore this trend. As a result this corporation does not own any small local markets. Buying patterns also changed after World War II, and this was an additional blow to the terminal markets. Before and during the War, sellers would fatten cattle, hogs and sheep to make them look choice to the packer buyers. The market was slipping on fed steers because there was no way to guarantee that the beef would grade choice after processing. Buyers for supermarkets and chain stores do not have the necessary skill to judge whether a steer will grade choice. As these retail markets are only interested in meat graded choice, this circumstance has led to direct buying in which the packer sends a buyer directly to the feeder to buy stock guaranteed to grade choice which means to yield 51% or more of dressed meat. There is no longer a slaughter market for a good grade steer, and this type of animal is generally sold as a feeder. The cattle market is mostly composed of stockers and feeders and cows and bulls that go to the terminal markets. There is not much price change anywhere. The market on cows that are not choice, such as milked-out dairy cattle or aged-out stocker cows is the same all over America. Most of this class of animal is turned into hamburger, so it does not matter how the meat is graded. As this class of old cows generally has very little fat, fat that must be trimmed from choice grade meat is ground up with this meat, giving additional flavor to the finished ground product. As a result the ground product sells for from 65 cents to as much as $1.00 per pound in some areas. Once fat was a drag on the market, and usually went to a soap maker. Now none is thrown away.[17]

The Forth Worth *Livestock Reporter* was the first livestock paper to identify another new trend in the marketing of livestock — the movement of cattle from the Southeast to the West. Cattle in Florida, Georgia, Tennessee, and Louisiana are

Load of "modern day" longhorn steers in Commission Co.'s pens on the Fort Worth Livestock market awaiting sale about 1950. Steers came from Yates ranch, Marathon, Texas. Courtesy, T. B. Saunders III

moving to the Texas plains, New Mexico, Arizona and California.[18] Lee Perkins of Clarksville, Texas participates in this trend. He buys calves in Alabama, Georgia and Tennessee, and ships them to his center in Clarksville where he rests and vaccinates the stock. Then he farms the calves out to his customers who pasture the stock on rye grass during the winter and other crops during the spring and summer. When Perkins wants his calves delivered back to his center he contacts his producers. He processes them once more before shipping the calves to the feed lots of of the Texas Panhandle and the West.[19]

There were over forty commission companies at the Fort Worth Livestock Exchange in 1940.[20] When John M. Lewis, president of the Union Stockyards Co., came to Fort Worth in 1958, twenty-eight commission firms were still doing business. Now only thirteen firms remain. Lewis reduced ninety-eight acres of pens to fifty-five acres. He also replaced the stockyard working horses and mules with motorcycles.[21] Armour and Swift continued to support the stockyards until Armour and Co. closed their plant in August, 1962. Swift and Co. closed down eight years later in July, 1970.[22] It is a different sort of market now. For example, Armour would not buy any sheep while Swift was still at Fort Worth. During May, 1971, Swift opened a plant at Brownwood,

104

Texas, and Armour is now back at Fort Worth to buy 350 to 400 sheep a week.[23] Finally in 1959, Fort Worth realized the need for an auction at a terminal market and one went into operation at the stockyards. The Fort Worth market is trying to maintain the strength and service of a terminal market, while offering the convenience and economy of the local sale to the farmer and stockman; and the lesson learned seems to be that it is no longer necessary to have a packing plant next door in order to run a successful livestock markket.

[1]Bertram B. Fowler, *Mean, Meat and Miracles* (New York: Julian Messner, Inc., 1952), pp. 27-28.

[2]J. Odgen Armour, *The Packers, The Private Car Lines And The People* (Philadelphia: Henry Altemus Company, June, 1906), p. 124.

[3]Fowler, *Men, Meat and Miracles*, pp. 28-35.

[4]Armour, *The Packers, The Private Car Lines And The People*, pp. 116-117.

[5]Paddock, *Early Days In Fort Worth*, p. 19.

[6]"Farm and Ranch," Fort Worth's First 100 Years, p. 2.

[7]*Fort Worth Star-Telegram*, Fort Worth, Texas. November 29, 1970, Section E, p. 1.

[8]Ted Gouldy. Interview at the office of the *Livestock Reporter*, Fort Worth, Texas, June 24, 1971.

[9]The Packer and Stockyards Act was ammended in 1940 so that a commission man could no longer be an agent for both buyer and seller.

[10]Ted Gouldy, *The Greater Southwest Livestock Sales* (Fort Worth: The Great Southwest Livestock Sales Corporation, about 1943).

[11]Gouldy. Interview at the office of the *Livestock Reporter*, Fort Worth, Texas, June 24, 1971.

[12]Gouldy, *The Greater Southwest Livestock Sales*.

[13]Ben K. Green. Interview at the office of the *Livestock Reporter*, Fort Worth, Texas, June 24, 1971.

[14]See old-crop lambs in Glossary.

[15]Proper guidelines for grading lambs are the look of the mouth and whether or not the carcass breaks at the joints.

[16]Gouldy. Interview at the office of the *Livestock Reporter*, Fort Worth, Texas, June 24, 1971.

[17]Gouldy and Green. Interiview at the office of the *Livestock Reporter*, Fort Worth, Texas, June 24, 1971.

[18]Gouldy. Interview at the office of the *Livestock Reporter*, Fort Worth, Texas, June 24, 1971.

[19]*Dallas Morning News*, Dallas, Texas. March 19, 1972, p. 36.

[20]40th Annual Report of the Fort Worth Stockyards Company for 1941.

[21]*Dallas Morning News*, Dallas, Texas. March 19, 1972, p. 36.

[22]*Actionorth*, Fort Worth, Texas, June, 1971.

[23]Bob Bramlett. Interview at the office of the *Livestock Reporter*, Fort Worth, Texas, June 24, 1971.

Selected Bibliography

I
Federal Laws and Documents

Corpus Juris Secundum — Volume 15, pp. 614-615.

Public Act No. 247. Laws Relating to Agriculture. U.S. Government Printing Office, Washington, D.C., 1971.

Public Law No. 41, Gilman G. Udell, Superintendent, Document Room, House of Representatives, U.S. Government Printing Office, Washington, D.C., 1971.

Public Law No. 51, Gilman G. Udell, Superintendent, Document Room, House of Representatives, U.S. Government Printing Office, Washington, D.C., 1971.

II
Cases Cited

Carter v. United States, C. A. A., Ga., 38F. (2d), 227.

Thorton v. United States, C. C. A., Fla., 2F. (2d), 561.

United States v. Texas, 162 United States, 1.

108

III
Interviews

Bramlett, Bob, Fort Worth, Texas.
Gouldy, Ted, Fort Worth, Texas.
Green, Dr. Ben K., Fort Worth, Texas.
Saunders, Tom, Fort Worth, Texas.
Voelkel, Dutch, Fort Worth, Texas.

IV
Newspapers

Dallas Morning News, Dallas, Texas, (March 19, 1972), p. 36.

Democrat, Fort Worth, Texas, 1873-1877.

Fort Worth Daily Livestock Reporter, Fort Worth, Texas, 1915, 1921, 1924, 1934.

Fort Worth Press, Fort Worth, Texas, 1936. "Texas Centennial Scrap Book Edition."

Fort Worth Record, Fort Worth, Texas, 1914, 1915.

Fort Worth Star-Telegram, Fort Worth, Texas, (October 30, 1949). "Fort Worth's First 100 Years." and (November 29, 1970).

Register, Fort Worth, Texas, (October 8, 1901), p. 11.

Weekly Citizen, Fort Worth, Texas, (May 18, 1906), p. 5.

V
Periodicals

"A Plan for a Dipping Vat," *The Cattleman.* (June, 1915), p. 17.

Boog-Scott, J. E., "Fever Tick Eradication in Texas," *The Cattleman.* (August, 1923), p. 41.

"Consider the Tick — May be Eradicated by Systematic Dipping," *The Cattleman.* (August, 1915), p. 16.

"Dr. Mark Francis," *The Cattleman.* (September, 1938), p. 13.

"Many Cattle Vaccinated at A & M College," *The Cat-*

tleman. (April, 1916), p. 55.

McClum, C. Boone, "History of the Manufacture of Barbed Wire," *Panhandle-Plains Historical Review.* (1958), pp. 17-26.

Moses, Dayton, Jr., "Texas Begins Last Fever Tick Drive," *The Cattleman.* (February, 1922), p. 15.

_____., "Tick Eradication in Texas," *The Cattleman.* (March, 1921), p. 223.

"New Restrictions on Tick Cattle," *The Cattleman.* (July, 1916), p. 39.

Nighbert, Dr. E. M., "The Importance of Tick Eradication," *The Cattleman.* (October, 1914), pp. 3-4.

"Oklahoma Puts Ban on Movement of Ticky Cattle," *The Cattleman.* (September, 1921), p. 33.

Saunders and Pattie, "Equinine Employes," *The Cattleman.* (September, 1970), p. 53.

Sim, William, "Tick Eradication at Texas A & M," *The Cattleman.* (January, 1923), p. 15.

"Summary of Tick Eradication in Texas in 1922," *The Cattleman.* (January, 1923), p. 32.

"Texas Campaign," *The Cattleman.* (June, 1922), p. 31

"Texas Tick Eradication Law Amended," *The Cattleman.* (June, 1920), p. 39.

The Cattleman, Volume II, No. 1. (June, 1915), p. 6.

"Tick Fever Studies Were a Boon to Mankind," *The Cattleman.* (March, 1930), pp. 54-55.

"Tick Infested Cattle Barred by Arkansas," *The Cattleman.* (December, 1921), p. 3.

"Ticky Cattle Barred From Maryland by Board Order," *The Cattleman.* (August, 1921), p. 10.

Wallace, W. A. "How to Get Best Results and Avoid Loss," *The Cattleman.* (July, 1914;, p. 6.

_____. "Tick Eradication — How to Avoid Loss From Dipping," *The Cattleman.* (July, 1915), p. 5.

"Will Make Claim Against Government for Damage to Cattle Dipped by Federal Inspector," *The Cattleman.* (December, 1915), p. 7.

110

VI
Miscellaneous

Actionorth, Fort Worth, Texas, June 24, 1971.

40th Annual Livestock Report of the Fort Worth Stock-yards Company for 1941.

Fort Worth Chamber of Commerce publication for 1938, available in the East Texas State University Library.

Fort Worth Chamber of Commerce, Fort Worth, Texas.

Gouldy, Ted, *The Greater Southwest Livestock Sales,* Fort Worth, about 1943.

Livestock Hotel, published by the Fort Worth Stock-yards Company about 1941.

Livestock Report of the Fort Worth Stockyards Company for 1915.

Paddock, Buckley B., *Early Days in Fort Worth, Much of Which I Saw and Part of Which I Was,* available in the archives of the Fort Worth Public Library.

Peak, Howard W., *The Story of Old Fort Worth,* available in the archives of the Fort Worth Public Library.

Rogers, Will., "Rogers Visits the Old Range," remarks to the Old Trail Drivers' Association. Copyright, 1926.

Royles, Milton C., "The Stockyard Story," available at the Fort Worth Chamber of Commerce.

Saunders, George W., Article prepared by the President, Old Trail Drivers' Association. Courtesy of his nephew, Tom Saunders.

"Texas In 3-D," *Kistler Graphics Inc.,* (1969), Denver, Colorado.

Texas Writers Project ("Research Data"), available in the Fort Worth Public Library.

VII
Books

Armour, J. Ogden, *The Packers, The Private Car Lines And The People,* Philadelphia: Henry Altemus Company, 1906.

Dale, Edward Everett, *The Range Cattle Industry,* Oklahoma: University of Oklahoma Press, 1930.

Douglas, C. L., *Cattle Kings of Texas,* Fort Worth: Branch-Smith, Inc., 1968.

Fowler, Bertram B., *Men, Meat and Miracles,* New York: Julian Messner, Inc., 1952.

Glover, Jack, *"Bubbed" Wire,* Wichita Falls: Terry Bros., Printers, 1966.

Green, Ben K., *Horse Tradin',* New York: Alfred A. Knopf, 1967.

————., *Wild Cow Trails,* New York: Alfred A. Knopf, 1969.

Knight, Oliver, *Fort Worth — Outpost on the Trinity,* Norman: University of Oklahoma Press, 1953.

McCallum, Henry D. and Frances T., *The Wire That Fenced The West,* Norman: University of Oklahoma Press, 1965.

Paddock, B. B., *Fort Worth and the Texas Northwest,* Vol. II of IV Volumes, Chicago: The Lewis Publishing Company, 1922.

Smith, Erwin E., *Life on the Texas Range,* Text by J. Evertts Haley, Austin: University of Texas Press, 1952.

Talbert, Robert Harris, *Cowtown-Metropolis,* Fort Worth: Texas Christian University, 1956.

Walker, Stanley, *Texas,* New York: The Viking Press, 1962.

112

Appendix

Glossary of Livestock Marketing Terms

Broker firm: is a clearing house for traders and speculators. The broker firm handles the business connected with clearance for the trader. It may put up loans and furnish the necessary bookkeeping services for a stockyards speculator not connected with a particular firm. Generally a broker charges a flat rate per head for the services of his office.

Cake fed: applies to stock which are pastured and given a supplementary feeding of compressed protein cubes made from high protein meals such as cottonseed, peanut or soya bean meal.

Cow market: can be a general term in reference to all kinds and grades of cattle, or it can refer specifically to cows.

113

Commission man: is a bonded agent of a commission firm. A stockman who wishes to sell his stock at a terminal market consigns his sheep to a commission man. Consignment means the seller may not prevent the commissioner from selling even though prices may be poor. The legal responsibility of consignment compels the commissioner to deposit the money received from selling his client's stock in a trust fund after he has deducted the commission and yard expenses. The commissioner cannot write a check on a trust account except to pay the seller for his livestock. His job is to advise the stockman as to the value of his stock and the best time to ship. From the time of shipment, the commissioner is responsible for seeing that the stock he receives is properly fed, watered and penned in his company's pens at the yards. He offers the consignment for sale always trying to secure the best possible price for the producer.

Creep feeding: is accomplished by building a feed dispenser with an over head storage area referred to as a hopper. A small enclosure is constructed around the hopper and feed trough which is large enough to permit calves to enter to eat, but too small to permit cows and larger stock to enter the enclosure.

Feeders: Stockers that are sufficiently mature to be placed in feed lots in order to finish them prior to slaughter.

Old-crop lambs: Last years' lambs which are ready to shed baby teeth. They are between new-crop lambs and yearlings. The classification is for butchering and feeder purposes.

Order buyer: an expert in his field. His services are available to purchasers who want expert representation in the procurement of a particular class of livestock. Doctors, lawyers and other professional people who cannot keep

114

posted on the market and do not have this kind of skill, use an order buyer. He is an agent who must be registered and bonded if he is working on a public stockyard.

Packer buyer: a buyer who represents a firm such as Swift. he buys with an eye for the dressed carcass and the quality of meat the animal will produce. He must be able to estimate the percentage yield of the carcass and guess the weight of the animal to within ten pounds after dress.

Price basing point: If a market has sufficient volume, it is a price basing point. If it does not then whatever happens on that market is only of local significance.

Private treaty: A man comes to a stockyard to buy stock. The stock for sale at the yards must be consigned to a commission firm which acts as an agent for the stock owner. The buyer does not have to be represented and may act as a private individual. The sale is negotiated between the buyer and a commission man who represents the seller.

Public auction: the opposite of private treaty. Stock is shown in an auction ring and offered for sale to the highest bidder. Anyone may attend the sales and bid. Auctions came to stockyards and terminal markets after World War II.

Stockers: Livestock that are generally returned to the country for breeding purposes or additional growth and weight gain.

Acknowledgments

The author of this study is indebted to many people for information and assistance. Only a few may be mentioned. Special gratitude is due Ben K. Green for his expert knowledge of the subject, his careful scrutiny of this book, and his helpful criticisms. This author wishes to thank Dr. Green most gratefully for permitting tapes to be made of his interviews with men involved in the marketing of livestock at Fort Worth. Special thanks is due Ted Gouldy who hosted the interviews at the office of the *Livestock Reporter* at Fort Worth on June 24, 1971. The author wishes to thank Ted Gouldy, Tom Saunders, Dutch Voelkel and Bob Bramlett for graciously consenting to be interviewed.